Selling to Builders

Steve Monroe

Home Builder Press®
National Association of Home Builders
1201 15th Street, NW
Washington, DC 20005-2800
(800) 223-2665
www.builderbooks.com

Selling to Builders
ISBN 0-86718-520-1

© 2001 by Home Builder Press®
of the National Association of Home Builders
of the United States of America

Library of Congress Cataloging-in-Publication Data
Monroe, Steve.
   Selling to Builders / Steve Monroe
     p.   cm.
   ISBN 0-86718-520-1 (pbk. : alk. paper)
     1. Building materials—Marketing.   2. Building fittings—Marketing   3.
Building materials industry—Customer services.   4. Building fittings industry—
Customer services.   5. Customer loyalty.   I. Title.

HD9715.8.A2 M66 2000
691'.068'8—dc21   00-048049

Disclaimer

For further information, please contact:

Home Builder Press®
National Association of Home Builders
1201 15th Street, NW
Washington, DC 20005-2800
(800) 223-2665
Check us out online at: www.builderbooks.com

11/00 Circle Graphics/ P.A. Hutchinson 2000

Contents

Figures   **v**

About the Author   **vi**

Acknowledgments   **vii**

Introduction   **1**

1 An Overview of the Builder Market   **3**
What This Information Does for You   **6**
General Characteristics of Builders   **7**

2 Assess Your Strengths   **13**
A Place to Begin   **13**
Assessing Your Endurance   **17**
When Are You Most Productive?   **18**
What Do You Really Do?   **19**
Goal Setting   **21**

3 Build a Plan of Action   **27**
A Guide to the Personal Sales Planner   **28**
Current Builder Base Profile   **32**
Choosing New Products   **32**
Growth Plans   **34**
Get the Builder Involved   **36**
Other Sources of Information   **38**
Get the Word Out   **39**
Putting Your Personal Sales Planner to Work   **40**
Opening New Territories   **41**

4 Help Build Your Company for the Future   43
Sales Support Staff   43

5 Meet the Competition Head On   49
Step 1. Getting to Know Them   49
Step 2. Field Assessment   50

6 The Sale   55
Basic Selling Techniques   56
Presentation Preparation for Medium- and
    Large-Volume Builders   64
The Presentation   65
Negotiation   67
The Close   69
Price, Product, or Service   70
The Second Sales Call   71
Future Buying Trends   72

7 Build Territorial Management Skills   73
Relationships?   73
The Client Management Folder   75
Planning for a Successful Week   78
Territorial Management   81

8 Build a Career-Friendly Network   85
Characteristics of Reliable Network People   87
A Resource Schedule For Leads   87

9 Working with Large-Volume Builders   93

10 Some Last Thoughts   99
When the Wheels Fall Off   99
"Wow, We Do Have a Problem"   100
Simple Steps to Solving Problems   102
Time Is Everything   103
Set Limits: When Enough is Enough   103
Making the Most of Your Local Home Builders
    Association Membership   104
Maximize Your Outside Resources: Work with
    Manufacturer's Representatives   105
A Good Ride   107

Notes   109

Figures

Chapter 1: An Overview of the Builder Market

1.1   Primary Business Activity of the Firm   **4**
1.2   Other Important Activities of the Firm   **5**
1.3   Time Line for Construction of a Home   **10**

Chapter 2: Assess Your Strengths

2.1   Successful Sales Attitude/Behavior Inventory—Self   **14**
2.2   Successful Sales Attitude/Behavior Inventory—Coworker   **15**
2.3   Successful Sales Attitude/Behavior Inventory—Customer   **16**
2.4   Time Tracker   **22**
2.5   Time Chart for Goals   **25**

Chapter 3: Build a Plan of Action

3.1   The Personal Sales Planner   **28**
3.2   Partnership Agreement   **37**

Chapter 4: Help Build Your Company for the Future

4.1   Critical Needs Schedule   **45**

Chapter 5: Meet the Competition Head On

5.1   Competitor Checklist   **51**
5.2   Today I Made Life Interesting For My Competitors By . . .   **53**

Chapter 6: The Sale

6.1   Effective Sales Kit Checklist   **57**
6.2   Sales Approaches by Volume   **57**
6.3   Quick Quote Form   **60**
6.4   Prospective Customer Sheet   **62**

Chapter 7: Build Territorial Management Skills

7.1   The Client Management Folder   **76**
7.2   Time Chart   **80**
7.3   Weekly Schedule   **82**
7.4   The Value of Your Time   **83**

Chapter 8: Build a Career-Friendly Network

8.1   Leads Notice   **90**

About the Author

Steve Monroe is a veteran sales and sales management professional in the building supplies and contract sales industry, who has served new home construction builders for three decades. To use his sales experience to assist others, he founded SME and Associates of Jamestown, North Carolina, a consulting and marketing firm. Under the SME "umbrella," he speaks to suppliers and professional builder networks, conducts sales training and human relations workshops, and writes related material for local and state trade association publications. Monroe also has made presentations to civic and community organizations, as well as local community colleges. He is the editor and publisher of *The Monroe Doctrine*, a newsletter for professionals in sales and management. He is listed in *Who's Who In Professional Speaking* and is a member of the National Speakers Association.

Currently also employed by Plyler Supply, an exterior material supplier for the Triad area of North Carolina (West Salem, High Point, and Greensboro). Monroe serves two local home builder associations (HBAs) in various capacities. His innovations for Triad area HBAs include a formal New Member Orientation Program and the inception of Builders' Expo, a regional trade show. He has been a North Carolina State Director.

Before moving to North Carolina, Monroe worked with builders in the Columbus, Ohio; Chicago; and Lexington, Kentucky, areas as a representative of companies providing premium materials to the building industry, including 15 years with Sears Contract Sales. He worked with the builder associations in each of those locales, and the companies also provided substantial support for these professional builder associations.

Monroe has been named Associate of the Year three times by local home builders associations and was a nominee from North Carolina as National Associate of the Year.

Acknowledgments

Some readers think that authors sit down with pad and pen or with a laptop and the words leap to on the page or screen and people read the book. Wrong! This book utilized the talents and time of a good number of gifted friends:

- Linda Hobson for taking sketches of forms and creating many forms that are used in the text, plus making the challenge of working with a new computer so much easier that it could have been.
- Susan Crawford, Ph.D., who made the simple idea of a survey of needs into a workable idea that made it to the Web. She took the raw data and compiled it to make sense for those who would read and benefit from the knowledge. Dr. Crawford also crafted the self-assessment devices used in Chapter 2.
- The Executive Officers in selected cities who shared the survey with their builder members, and those builder members who took the time to respond by mail or by the Web.
- Sandy Parrott, Greater Greensboro Builders Association, and Janice Arrowood, High Point Builders Association who listened and suggested during the research and writing process.
- Ginny Etter of the GGBA staff who never ran when I showed up and needed something done regarding the computer.
- Doris M. Tennyson, Senior Acquisitions Editor of Home Builder Press, National Association of Home Builders, whose patience and prompting kept me on task.
- Michelle Robbins, who made the final tweaks and suggestions that have made this book a much better read.
- Reagan Suggs and Joann Gattis, who read and suggested changes to the text.
- Bill Moore, the most creative person that I know, who urged me to quit talking about writing a book and do it.

- My best friend and wife, Louise, who read, cajoled, encouraged, and listened during the whole process.
- My daughter-by-marriage, Rebecca Chadwick, who patiently added details to the text and made last-minute forms appear from napkins.
- The large number of sales professionals I have been privileged to work with: Lynn Heller, a fine example of how to be organized and successful; Bob Morreale, who shows how to keep the fire alive in sales while maintaining strong profits; Steve McClain, who combines the skills of the two previously mentioned individuals.
- David Cooper ,who has added new chapters in persistence and focus, and Zach Elkin who along with Bob Hatfield, have proved that you can be successful in both sales and management.
- Members of my network who keep the contacts coming: Scott Shina, Tim Crawford, Patricia Trippe, Ken Martin, Harry Bleattler, Jr., John Hamrick, Mark Whitehouse, Fred Philips, Larry Hall, and Tommy Adams.
- Chris Plyler, a true entrepreneur, who still believes in the principle of bottom-up management and has been proven right.
- The entire sales team at Plyler Supply Company, Inc., Winston-Salem branch, who make my life interesting and selling to builders a success: Carol, Jodi, Mike, William, Wayne, Scott, Russell, Ismael, Tom and Christina.
- The thousands of builders it has been my privilege to work with over the years. You have provided the understanding of and insight into how to work effectively with builders.

Reviewers

The following people reviewed the outline and/or all or part of the manuscript for *Selling to Builders:* Kelly Bakane, 2000 NAHB Associate Member Committee, Sears Contract Sales, Hoover, Alabama; Shawn Draper, Metallon, Inc., Parkersburg, West Virginia; Roger Frisman, 1997–98 NAHB Associate Members Committee, Midland Title Security, Inc. Cleveland, Ohio; Ralph O. Kennedy, II, 2000 NAHB Associate Members Committee, Evans Title Companies, Inc., Appleton, Wisconsin; Harold McCracken, 1997–98 NAHB Associate Members Committee, Lexington, Kentucky; Darryl L. Mancini, 1997–98 NAHB Associate Members Committee, United Underwriters, Broadview Heights, Ohio; Meg Meyer, Executive Director, NAHB's National Sales and Marketing Council, Washington, D.C.; Jerry Neese, 1997–98 NAHB Associate Members Committee, Georgia Power Company, Atlanta, Georgia; E. Lee Reid, Reid Homes and Real Estate, Apollo Beach, Florida; Jerry Strebel, 1997–98 NAHB Associate Members Committee, GE Appliances, Brentwood, Tennessee; and Lee Terry, 2000 NAHB Associate Members Committee, Lee Terry and Associates, San Mateo, California; Julia Baron, Director, NAHB Associate Member Programs, Washington, D.C.

Book Preparation

Selling to Builders is produced under the general direction of Jerry Howard, NAHB Executive Vice President and CEO, in association with NAHB staff members Rob Pflieger, Senior Staff President, Public Affairs; Greg French, Assistant Staff Vice President, Public Affairs; Charlotte McKamy, Publisher, Home Builder Press; Doris M. Tennyson, Senior Acquisitions Editor; Andy Schwarz, Director of Sales and Marketing; David Rhodes, Art and Production Director; and Toral Patel, Assistant Editor.

Introduction

It looked so easy. My driving companion got out of his car, then half walked, half leaped across a ditch at the job site. He stepped nimbly around and over plywood, 2 × 4's, and blackboard until he got to the house under construction. Looking around, he spotted someone who to him looked like a builder. Festooned in dark blue blazer and gray trousers, with patent leather shoes that allowed for quick cleanups, he stuck out his hand and told the builder his name and affiliation.

"Anybody could do this," I thought. Little did I understand how much you need to know to sell successfully to builders. My friend knew, and as with all true professionals, he made it look easy.

This book shares lessons I've learned from observation, application, and mistakes—and the wisdom gained from all three. It has been my privilege to sell to builders for more than 25 years. The systematic approach described here grew out of an appreciation not just for what it takes to be successful but for what it takes to apply the principles that lead to success.

The system began to take formal shape several years ago as I pulled together a training regime to both help new people joining my sales team and to enhance the performance of those already on board. It's a system that contains a sufficient number of forms as part of its methodology.

Believe me, I'm more than aware that good salespeople hate forms and paperwork in general, so use what you will. The system has been used with success by others, but like anything else of worth that has been tried, it will only work if used. If you find only one section that fits what you need, then the book has been of value. Use it and be successful.

1

An Overview
of the Builder
Market

Ask a builder why he or she chose that profession, and you're likely to get variety of answers. The response would be tempered by the weather, the mood of the current client, the builder's experience, or long-term interest rates. Look beyond everyday concerns about a lack of dependable labor, the need for better prices from suppliers, and the scarcity of easily buildable lots, and you find a person of vision. A builder has the gift to see substance where others see only raw land, opportunity where others see obstacles. And, the successful ones do it while posting a profit.

Builders may be among the last of the risk takers in America, and they lead the charge when it comes to optimism. Imagine taking a concept that begins totally in one's mind, putting it on paper, committing that concept to a blueprint, and then seeing that blueprint through the local government's building review committee. If the plan makes it that far, the builder sets the footprint on a piece of land, prepares the site, and begins building, ultimately giving form to an image that began in his or her mind. But more than an idea or concept is at risk. The process is the same when a builder must take a picture that exists only in the mind of a prospective homeowner and give it a specific shape. The builder puts both personal and financial capital on the line (including his or her reputation and esteem) in hopes that a family will be pleased enough to purchase the home and share their delight with family and friends.

Selling to builders or servicing their needs allows you to be part of this fast-paced, creative world. But which kind of builders or which aspect of the building industry should you target? The charts in Figures 1.1 and 1.2 will help you understand the various types of builders and their areas of business emphasis.

These groups serve as the National Association of Home Builders' marking points for the classification of builders. You may choose to tailor your goods and services by taking into consideration the number of units produced by a given builder. Some build only a few extremely expensive homes, but their total volume might equal that

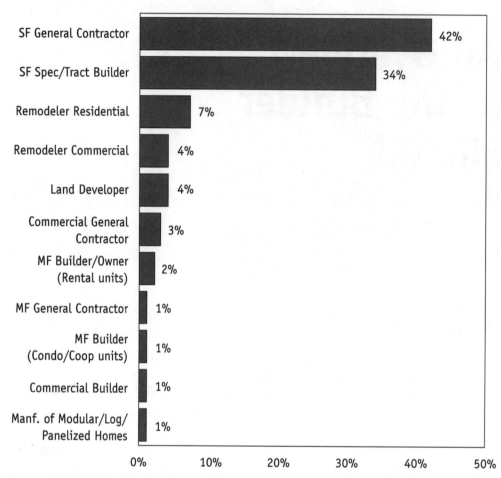

FIGURE 1.1 Primary Business Activity of the Firm

Percent of Respondents

Source: NAHB Builder Member Census.

of a small production builder. You decide what is important to you in establishing prices for your goods and services.

For this book I classify builders by the number of units they produce in a year. Dollar volume is a strong indicator of a builder's presence in the market but so is the number of actual units built. What you offer in goods and services reflects which factor is more important to you. If you are in the business of supplying material or contract services to a builder, the number of units he or she will build yearly is critical. If you supply services that aid the building process—accounting or marketing support, computers, home sales, or mortgages, for instance—volume may not be so important. Often the number of units constructed helps determine not only price but whether the supplier or trade contractor can meet the needs of the builder. Buying habits and a more detailed description of these builders are found in Chapter 6.

Of the 133,976 associate members of NAHB, there are 57,398 builders with an average of 13 years in business. They purchase more than $55 billion in building materials each year and employ more than 1.1 million people. Add to that total the $45 bil-

FIGURE 1.2 Other Important Activities of the Firm

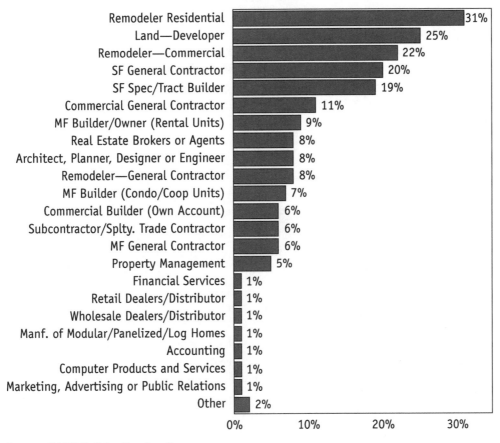

Percent of Respondents

Source: NAHB Builder Member Census.

lion spent annually by remodelers, and your potential market is enormous by anyone's standards. And those figures are just for material.

Not only is the industry large, but builders take their finished product to market in a variety of ways. NAHB describes builders by classifying each by sales volume (average sale price) and by type. These classifications, which have different purchasing and service requirements, determine what you can sell in service and/or products. In June 1999 a census survey of NAHB builder members (169,500 responding) showed the following breakdown by volume:

- Small-volume builders (10 starts a year or fewer) constituted 4 percent of the homes built by NAHB members.
- Moderate-volume builders reported 11 to 25 starts a year and built 13 percent of the homes.
- Medium-size builders reported 26 to 100 homes per year and were responsible for 44 percent of the homes started.
- Large-volume builders reported starts that exceed 100 units per year; they accounted for 39 percent of the total volume.

Small- and moderate-volume builders often use standard plans that can be modified to suit the needs of a client. These builders often purchase scattered lots in a development from another builder or developer. The moderate-volume builder may employ a jobsite supervisor who takes care of day-to-day detail; small-volume builders usually run the job themselves.

Small- or moderate-volume builders could also have a small development of their own of 10 acres or less, depending on local building restrictions. Most of the building activity is financed by the builder or through local financial institutions. The builder does some marketing, but he or she often gains referrals from clients or works through a real estate broker.

Production builders, called large-volume or tract builders, produce attached and detached single-family homes from standard plans with the possibility of minor modifications. They may sell these homes prior to construction or build them on a speculative basis. Medium- and large-volume builders are included in this category. Using computer-generated production systems, a superintendent (often called a builder) is managed by regional representatives of the home office.

This type of operation impacts the speed of construction as well as the need to have great communication links with all concerned in the process. Other parts of the company that are impacted by this process are the estimating, marketing, and purchasing departments. Lending is generally project-based, although some large-volume builders are self-funded. Sales are conducted from the models in each development, often using in-house salespeople. Production builders normally are involved in land purchases and development and work several years ahead of current demand.

Production builders may have a home office and regional branches supervised by superintendents (also called builders) using computer-generated production systems. While not included in the survey I conducted in conjunction with researching this book, custom builders construct one-of-a-kind homes for specific clients. They often build in upscale developments on scattered sites using a jobsite superintendent. They depend on the real estate community to supply leads and use referrals from homeowners. The price for their homes often exceeds $500,000.

But not all builders concentrate on single-family homes. Some derive all or a portion of their yearly sales from remodeling. Others serve as general contractors, devoting most of their resources to building and developing multifamily projects such as apartments, condominiums, and town homes, or commercial properties such as small shopping centers, offices, and/or warehouse complexes.

What This Information Does for You

Take a few minutes to look beyond the general information given in the charts. They provide an overall indication of the national building picture, but your market and your builder base will vary. Those variances will be more than just size or geographical area. Economic forces and the movement of the general population can have a definite impact. Change is a constant factor, a dynamic that can make your career interesting and work in this industry fun.

Use the following questions to measure how your market has changed.

- Who were the leaders in your local market 10 years ago?
- Who arrived during that period and who left?

- What factors led to the moves? Adding to the equation are the availability and affordability of lots, sufficient water, expansion of wastewater capability, and the addition or loss of jobs.
- Have new or improved highways come to your area in the last five years? Where will new or improved highways be built in the next five years?
- For the last several years, nationally known builders have ventured from their established bases and have expanded by acquiring major players in local markets. Has this happened in your area?

Change also occurs in your area of expertise. Look at the products sold to builders. Virtually any item that involves computers did not exist before the early 1990s. With the addition of lasers, even the vital task of laying out the footprint of a house has become a one-person job.

The explosion in the use of cellular telephones has allowed builders and suppliers to be readily accessible, even while on a jobsite. Laminated veneer lumber (LVL) has revolutionized the framing process. The advent of oriented strand board (OSB) has impacted exterior walls from medium-density fiberboard (MDF) to basic trim packages. One manufacturer of vinyl siding is close to producing a system that will allow the builder to hang vinyl siding and the needed structural material for an exterior wall in the same operation. Composite materials are becoming commonplace while state-of-the-art computers help homeowners deal with rising energy costs. Smart House® technology is now available across the country, and more and more builders are advertising their products on the Internet. Some builders have stopped constructing a series of model homes in a development in favor of virtual reality showrooms.

Regardless of the dynamics of change, builders still construct houses, and their businesses still have several characteristics in common.

General Characteristics of Builders

- In my experience, many building firms are family-centered organizations; you can easily find several generations working on the same jobsite. Father passes to son or daughter who then passes to son or daughter. At a recent meeting in Kentucky, a builder I have known for 20 years told me his son was joining his company and I could see the pride shining in his eyes. This trend is not unique to just small- and medium-volume builders. Many of the largest building concerns in the United States have their roots in family-oriented businesses.
- A builder is a fiercely independent-thinking entrepreneur in the styles of houses constructed, the location of those houses, and the ability to react quickly to market changes.
- A builder and his or her support staff (sales, field, and clerical) need more information and education than ever. Every day they face an increasing array of products and services to assist them in constructing homes, and they face well-informed consumers who know how to ask tough questions. The builder's staff must answer those questions quickly and with confidence.
- Because a home is the single biggest investment that most families make, a builder must construct a home that meets their expectations. What can you do, supply, or install that will help the builder do this.

- An increasing number of fees and regulations slow down the construction schedule and add more cost to a house. NAHB estimates that 23 percent of the cost of an average house goes to satisfy regulations, up from 9 percent in 1975. Being an NAHB builder member does not insulate builders from this increasing demand. It just gives them a more pronounced and louder voice when decisions are made.

- Builders are high maintenance from a service standpoint. Because many of them use the just-in-time approach when ordering materials, suppliers must be capable of responding immediately to requests. Even with the introduction of computer-assisted design (CAD) plans and the building schedules they produce, builders still have last-minute requests. They will need fill-in material because of new crews, shrinkage, or changes from the homeowner-to-be. Your response time will be key to gaining and keeping a builder's business as well as his or her confidence.

- As critical as service is, price remains an issue. The pressure is ever-present for builders to stay within budget. For production builders, the cost constraints come from both superiors and shareholders. Price competition is fierce in this category, and many builders concentrate on providing as much product as they can per square foot. Deciding factors include location, features and benefits, and price per square foot. You can keep your price level competitive by knowing your competitors' prices and the weight their products carry in the marketplace. You need to know your products or services well enough to sell from a value-added position. (For more on knowing your competition, see Chapter 5.) What you offer the builder matters; a need or desire for the product or service then sets the demand in motion.

- Many builders dislike undertaking the uncertain, so they resist change. Your challenge as a salesperson or trade contractor is to give them reasons to do so. Take a moment or two and answer the following questions to determine your level of awareness of what you are offering. Consider whether you are giving prospective clients a reason to change.

  - Why should the builder change to use your services?
  - Do you offer more efficient deliveries of products?
  - Do you have in-house design services?
  - What commitment have you made to establishing or maintaining deeper levels of inventory?
  - Do you have an in-house service department?
  - Do you offer greater value for service delivered?
  - Do you offer a greater degree of reliability in the delivery or performance of the product?
  - Do you offer faster callbacks and on-time crews?

In every business relationship, difficulties occur over time. Whether the challenge is a lost order, a missed delivery, or a resistant back order, the attitude you and your company take in solving the problem will strengthen or break the relationship.

- Builders, as a general rule, are proud of their products, regardless of square footage. Whether that product takes the form of starter homes or the grandest houses in the market, builders hold their work to their own high standards.

- Builders who stay ahead of the curve modify their building practices and organizations in response to changes in the culture in which they build. One of those changes occurring now is the influx of people moving to the United States to work-and to purchase homes. You may need to learn a second language to converse with trade contractors or some of a builder's employees.
- Another change in the building scene in many markets is the introduction of national large-volume builders. Many of these respected firms come to new markets and obtain immediate market share by purchasing local or regional building companies.
- With an influx of national large-volume builders into small and medium markets, local small-volume builders are scrambling to find lots and meet the price points the new competition brings to town.
- The United States was once a nation of regional cultures, which allowed builders to design products for their own well-established market. Now, however, companies move employees from region to region on a regular basis. The South, for instance, is no longer populated by people raised there. It has grown significantly thanks to an influx of people transferred from the East and Midwest. Successful builders are adapting to the expectations that new buyers bring.
- Don't stereotype. Not all builders are men who wear khaki trousers and drive pick up trucks. I was reminded of this fact on a recent sales call to a builder whose sign bore only initials. As I approached the two people applying a hardwood floor over underlayment, I greeted both parties then began speaking directly to the gray-haired man, not the young woman using the air hammer. I soon learned that the A in A.L. stood for Amber. Don't assume.
- According to the U.S. Census Bureau report on women-owned businesses, women are the principle owners in 230,000 construction businesses. An additional 603,000 women were reported being employed in the industry in 1996. Of those, 22 percent worked for home builders and 56 percent for trade contractors.
- In the fast-paced building environment, the ability to deliver a product or service on time and within budget remains a major consideration for builders. Price or brand name are of little value if goods cannot be where they are needed in a timely fashion. Builders are in a constant race with the weather and time. They cannot control what nature brings, but they can exert some control over their schedules. If your driver misses a delivery on Friday, or your crew takes a couple days off when it's needed to finish a job for a builder, you cost the builder time, a commodity he or she cannot replace. Builders get no days off from interest on construction loans or from clients' expectations. Keep those two points in mind, and you'll take a giant step forward in identifying and meeting builders' needs.

The time line in Figure 1.3 shows the building process and your place as a provider of goods and services along a time line. Your ability to anticipate when a builder will need you enhances your chances for success and helps ensure an invitation to be part of the next house. Being early works best in most cases. Weather permitting, a traditionally constructed two-story home can be built, on average, in the 90 to 120 days spanning dates 1 to 14 in Figure 1.3.

FIGURE 1.3 Time Line for Construction of a Home

Time	Task	Service/Product
PRIMARY STAGE		
Date 1	Find and purchase a suitable lot	Realtor®, developer, attorney, banker, networking by suppliers
Date 2	Discover or design a plan that can be built at a profit. "Do not build a monument to yourself" Sam Westbrook, Builder	Architect, house planner
Date 2	Find a prospect to buy the house	Realtor ®, network, in house sales Mortgage company, title company Advertising to public
FOUNDATION STAGE		
	Well/septic permit	Government
	Building permit	Government
	Water meters	Water authority
	Plans/printing	Blue print duplicator
	Well	Well driller
	Septic system	trade contractor
Date 3	Clear lot and layout footprint House staking	Surveyor, excavation crews
Date 4	Pour footer and lay foundation	Concrete, concrete finishers, brick and concrete masons
	Flat work/concrete	Masons
	Backfill	Landscaper
	Driveway stone	Quarry
	Fine grading	Landscaper
	Termite inspection	Trade contractor
	Brick foundation and materials	Masonry supplier
	Sand/gravel	Masonry supplier
	Block, mortar, ties, etc.	Masonry supplier
	Fireplace	Installed by supplier
	Brick veneer, loose brick, etc.	
	Waterproofing	Applied by trade contractor
DRYING IN STAGE		
Date 5	Build floor system	A. If slab, concrete needs to follow plumber. B. If wood, truss systems, lumber, framing carpenters.
Date 5	Wall systems	Lumber, fasteners, framers
Date 6	Roof or second floor	Lumber, trusses, framers, felt. Crane operators
	Structural steel	As per plan, it may need to be engineered by architect.
	Plywood/OSB	Lumber yard
	Insulation board	Lumber yard

FIGURE 1.3 Time Line for Construction of a Home (*Continued*)

Time	Task	Service/Product
DRYING IN STAGE (*Continued*)		
	Prefab stair units	Millwork company
	Soffit material	Lumber yard
	Exterior millwork	Lumber yard
	Porch material	Lumber yard
Date 7	Roof and mechanical rough-ins	Shingles, roofers, electricians, plumbers, Heating and Air
Date 8	Windows, exterior doors, vents Skylights	Framers, appropriate supplier
	Garage door	Applicator
Date 8a	Exterior finish	Appropriate product supplied and applied.
	Guttering	Gutter installer
	Splash blocks	Supplied by lumber yard
	Fine grading	Excavator
FINISHING STAGE		
Interior		
Date 9	Hardwood floor	Sand in place before drywall
Date 10	Drywall	Hangers and appropriate supplier
Date 11	Trim	Wood trim, finish carpenter, cabinets set plumbing fixtures, bath tile
	Painting	Painting contractor
Date 12	Interior Vanities/medicine cabinets Mirrors Wall covering Shower/bath accessories	Carpet, tile, appliances, light fixtures
Exterior		
Date 13	Back fill around foundation	Landscaper
	Deck material	Lumber yard, labor
	Wrought iron	
	Privacy fence	
	Shutters	
		Drive way, concrete/asphalt
		Sewer and water tap, plumber
	Storm drains	
	Landscaping, landscaper	
Date 14	Closing	Realtor®, attorney, title company Mortgage company

Use this typical schedule for building a house in determining where you fit in. When working with builders, always remember that more than just a schedule is at stake. Some goods and services are more critical than others. If you supply one of these, take heed. The most pressing need will be to meet the building inspector's schedule for the duration of the job. If you do not deliver or install your product or service when the builder needs it and the job is turned down by an inspector at any stage, delays occur all along the building process. The need to reschedule other trade contractors and suppliers will demand more time than the builder may have and will take time away from supervising other houses under construction.

For builders, of course, beneath their concerns about weather and schedules and permits lies an inherent pride in workmanship. Long-time builders will take you past homes and communities and proudly point out what they have done over the years. They will note how well the houses have stood the test of time, how they have made a positive difference in the areas in which they build. These houses are their legacy for generations to come, and the products and services you provide are a part of that. Welcome.

Assess Your Strengths

Now that you have a basic understanding of your customer—the builder—examine where you fit into the sales equation. You are the means your company has chosen to reach the builder. How equipped are you to handle the job?

A Place to Begin

The series of Sales Professional Profiles in this chapter are designed to help you examine the skills you bring to the marketplace. Take your time in answering them; the extra time will add value to this exercise. In one, you describe yourself. The second will help you evaluate how you are viewed by a peer in your role in selling to builders; the third gives you the builder's viewpoint. The perspective of others is valuable in forming a balanced view of your effectiveness as a sales or service professional. Be brave enough to allow both a close friend and a respected customer to fill out the comparison forms. Pick people one who will always tell you the truth, regardless of whether you want to hear it. Compare their responses to yours; theirs may provide fresh insight into how you are perceived in the marketplace (Figures 2.1, 2.2, and 2.3).

How did you do? Any surprises? New insights, perhaps? Valuable information results whenever we allow trusted colleagues to give us solid impressions about how we appear to them. What did your reviewers view as your greatest strength? What aspects of the "inventory" need to be enhanced? Address some of those needs by taking courses at a local community college or consider using an audio or video series. Have you researched and made plans to read books that address those issues? Look for books in your local library, bookstore, or on the Internet.

Decide that over the next six months you're going to read at least three books or review two tape or video series on the most pertinent issues you need to address. If you attend your state convention, the International Builders Show, or the National Kitchen and Bath Show, you may find some relevant seminars. The Remodel America

FIGURE 2.1 Successful Sales

Attitude/Behavior Inventory—Self

Your name:_____ Date:_____

Current position:_____

The following instrument has been designed to determine the sales profile of an individual salesperson. Please read the following statements and rate yourself on the listed criteria and be as candid as possible when completing the rating, as you may be interested in comparing the feedback you receive from others with your own perspective.

DIRECTIONS: Read the following statements about yourself. Think about all the situations in which you have found yourself and place a ✓ under the expression that best describes your response. If you have not encountered a specific situation, please check "Not Known." **When you have completed the rating, go back and place an ⊠ in the box beside all the characteristics you think are most important to good sales.**

	Never 0%	Rarely 1–25%	Sometimes 26–55%	Almost Always 56–84%	Always 85–100%	Not Known
❑ I return calls/pages in a timely fashion.						
❑ I pay attention to details, allowing little to "fall through the cracks."						
❑ I arrive on time.						
❑ I approach work in an organized fashion.						
❑ I have integrity.						
❑ I have a strong knowledge of the building market in the area.						
❑ I am aware of local conditions that affect the strength of the local market.						
❑ I am considered to be an expert in my field.						
❑ I am used as a consultant on specific projects.						
❑ I like people.						
❑ I have a positive attitude toward life.						
❑ I enjoy finding solutions to problems.						

On a scale of *one* to *five*, with *five* indicating a top salesperson, and *one* indicating someone who should find another profession, rank yourself compared with other top salespeople you have encountered. Please circle your choice: 1   2   3   4   5

Thank you for completing this inventory. Please return it to the person whom you were rating.

FIGURE 2.2 Successful Sales

Attitude/Behavior Inventory—Coworker

Your name:_____ Date: _____

Current position:_____ Person you are evaluating_____

What is your relationship to this person: _____

The following instrument has been designed to determine the sales profile of an individual salesperson. Please read the following statements and rate this person on the listed criteria and be as candid as possible when completing the rating, as the individual is interested in receiving feedback from a number of objective perspectives.

DIRECTIONS: Read the following statements about the person you are rating. Think about all the encounters you have had with this person with regard to the statement and place a ✓ under the expression that best describes them. If you have not encountered this individual in that specific situation, please check "Not Known." **When you have completed the rating, go back and place an ⊠ in the box beside all the characteristics you think are most important to good sales.**

This person:	Never 0%	Rarely 1–25%	Sometimes 26–55%	Almost Always 56–84%	Always 85–100%	Not Known
❏ Returns calls/pages in a timely fashion.						
❏ Pays attention to details, allowing little to "fall through the cracks."						
❏ Arrives on time.						
❏ Approaches work in an organized fashion.						
❏ Has integrity.						
❏ Has a strong knowledge of the building market in the area.						
❏ Is aware of local conditions that affect the strength of the local market.						
❏ Is considered to be an expert in my field.						
❏ Is used as a consultant on specific projects.						
❏ Appears to like people.						
❏ Appears to have a positive attitude toward life.						
❏ Enjoys finding solutions to problems.						

On a scale of *one* to *five*, with *five* indicating a top salesperson, and <u>one</u> indicating someone who should find another profession, rank yourself compared with other top salespeople you have encountered. Please circle your choice: 1   2   3   4   5

Thank you for completing this inventory. Please return it to the person whom you were rating.

FIGURE 2.3 Successful Sales

Attitude/Behavior Inventory—Customer

Your name:_____   Date: _____

Current position:_____   Person you are evaluating_____

What is your relationship to this person: _____

The following instrument has been designed to determine the sales profile of an individual salesperson. Please read the following statements and rate this person on the listed criteria and be as candid as possible when completing the rating, as the individual is interested in receiving feedback from a number of objective perspectives.

DIRECTIONS: Read the following statements about the person you are rating. Think about all the encounters you have had with this person with regard to the statement and place a ✓ under the expression that best describes them. If you have not encountered this individual in that specific situation, please check "Not Known." **When you have completed the rating, go back and place an ⊠ in the box beside all the characteristics you think are most important to good sales.**

This person:	Never 0%	Rarely 1–25%	Sometimes 26–55%	Almost Always 56–84%	Always 85–100%	Not Known
❑ Returns calls/pages in a timely fashion.						
❑ Pays attention to details, allowing little to "fall through the cracks."						
❑ Arrives on time.						
❑ Approaches work in an organized fashion.						
❑ Has integrity.						
❑ Has a strong knowledge of the building market in the area.						
❑ Is aware of local conditions that affect the strength of the local market.						
❑ Is considered to be an expert in my field.						
❑ Is used as a consultant on specific projects.						
❑ Appears to like people.						
❑ Appears to have a positive attitude toward life.						
❑ Enjoys finding solutions to problems.						

On a scale of *one* to *five*, with *five* indicating a top salesperson, and <u>one</u> indicating someone who should find another profession, rank yourself compared with other top salespeople you have encountered. Please circle your choice: 1   2   3   4   5

Thank you for completing this inventory. Please return it to the person whom you were rating.

Conference and Exhibition does a particularly effective job of presenting seminars for suppliers and trade contractors.

Regardless of how you choose to address the identified strengths and the improvements you need to make, the time and money you invest in your career will be well spent. You cannot measure every strength or weakness because of an "X-factor." You must decide how much you want the sale, the account, or the contract. What are you willing to expend in time, energy, and ethics to get what you want?

The atmosphere in which you present your product or service can be challenging. As a young sales manager, I went along with the regional salesperson to meet a well known and well respected prospective builder whom the salesperson had pursued for years. We entered his office and were greeted by a sign that read, "We shoot every third salesman, and the second one just left." It made us think: "How hungry were we to do business with this builder?" Were we prepared to do what was necessary to get and keep the business? The answer that day was yes. We made the necessary proposals and obtained the contract, then enjoyed a mutually profitable relationship for as long as I was in the territory.

Assessing Your Endurance

Two other personal factors come into play for the trade contractor, sales, or service professional. When do you hit the wall, that invisible but real barrier that comes to all people who push their human resources to the limit?

The Wall Theory came to me years ago while I was a college student and working nights on a production line manufacturing typewriters. The entire line was paid a good hourly wage and received super benefits. We also got bonuses when we hit certain levels of quality and production. Demand was so great for the product in those days that we could often work overtime. It was during those overtime hours that I began to formulate the Wall Theory. We would cease regular production after eight hours, take a 15-minute break, then resume work. Pay rates went up by 50 percent, but production fell to less than what was produced during the regular shift. We were tired, not as focused even with the break, and unable to keep the same pace for a 10- to 12-hour period. We had hit the wall.

When do you hit the wall? Is the answer different during the week than on the weekend? Do you add weekends to your schedule, or do you allow little time for leisure activities? We all can drive ourselves harder than we should, but we will eventually hit the wall. We may put in the hours, but production falls.

Salespeople I have talked to over the years who understand the wall say they are more productive when they step back for a time and do something different. They return with renewed energy and perhaps even renewed insight. Learn where your wall is and take steps not to hit it. Some symptoms I have found in discussions with others include:

- You lack concentration, make more mistakes, and have greatly reduced production.
- A reduction in energy. Even with boosts of caffeine, you still feel drained.
- You experience a loss of drive to complete the job in a way that meets your standards.

■ You find you need a lot of patience to deal with problems or energy to keep going toward a solution.

What do you do when you hit the wall? What is your strategy for dealing with the symptoms described above? Can you recall your childhood or watching children play? In their method of play they go from activity to activity, making games along the way. By changing emphasis, children can maintain enthusiasm and eliminate boredom. So can you. When you hit the wall, go do something different.

If you spend a great deal of time behind the wheel or at a desk, get some serious physical exercise. Walking is a good release; summer evenings spent in the pool are super. If you're usually athletic, grab a book or take a nap. The idea is to do the opposite of what you normally do.

Have you tried to run away? Movies provide a good release, particularly if you can go during the week.

As a sales, service, or trade professional, you and I are challenged to use our physical and mental attributes to our advantage. What you put in your body as fuel and how much sleep you obtain will determine how you perform.

When Are You Most Productive?

Try to decide the time of day when you are most effective in the various aspects of your job. Some people are morning persons, others do better in the afternoon or evening. Where do you fall? Knowing that allows you to plan your day more effectively. When are the hours that you seem to have more insight into problem solving? When are you best at presenting the goods or services you represent?

Knowing this about yourself and following a discipline gained from that insight will help you plan your week.

Now that you can appreciate who you are and where your strengths and the improvements you need to make are, begin to pull together a plan to use these skills to strengthen your stand with builders in your market.

Building on What You Have Learned

If you are in the early stages of your career, focus on where you want to be in five years. This plan is for building community, not a physical location. Breaking your personal development plan into six-month sections will allow you to watch your progress and make adjustments. Many community colleges have small business centers that offer a broad array of courses that may fit your needs on a continual basis. Stay in touch with the latest ideas being sold at your local bookstore.

Audio-visual companies produce a variety of videos, tapes, and CD's to keep you in touch with the changing world of sales. Use them. Stay alert as to the great possibilities in this ever-changing business.

With the rapid increase in the number of non-English-speaking people involved in residential construction, you may need to learn another language. According to a 1998 article in *Nation's Building News*, 14.4 percent of all construction jobs (a total of 832,476 positions) are held by workers born outside the United States. The majority of these workers are from Mexico (43.5 percent) and its neighbors to the south (30.0 percent)[1].

How good is your Spanish? Your Korean? If you work with immigrants and do not know their language, you are both at a disadvantage. Check your local community college for second language courses. Why not lead your local home builders association in establishing an English as a second language course for these key trade contractors and their employees?

If you currently hold specific certifications in your chosen field, how will you stay in touch with the latest updates in your area of expertise? What Continuing Education Units will you need to keep your certification? Where and when will you get them? Can you add a course or two and enhance your rating?

The Home Builders Institute (HBI), the education and training arm of the National Association of Home Builders (NAHB), and the NAHB Associate Members Committee developed a course of study for associate members similar to its Certified Graduate Builder, Certified Graduate Remodeler, and Certified Sales Professional programs. The Certified Graduate Associate Program will equip the participant with a greater knowledge of how to better serve their customers (mostly builders and remodelers). Contact HBI at (800) 795-7955 or (202) 371-0600 for details.

Regardless of education or experience, your real motivation to succeed needs to come from within you. It is the echo of the heart that begins with that first sale. "It was a great day. I closed the sale!" "I finally got the builder to use me as his or her plumber." The rush that comes with success never leaves those who are true to their sales motivation.

What Do You Really Do?

When was the last time someone asked, "So, what do you do for a living?" Did you say: "I sell lumber," "I sell building materials," "I am a finish carpenter," "I provide financing," "I make insurance available for builders," or "I support those who use CAD systems." Is that really what you do? Broaden your perspective and see where you fit into the building of homes for millions of families.

People who sell vehicles don't sell cars, they sell luxury. A strong brand name sells prestige. Pizza takeout and delivery companies don't sell pizza; they sell convenience. Well known photographic film companies don't sell cameras or film, they sell memories. Do you sell computers to builders or do you sell them state-of-the-art communication devices? So, what do you really do for a living?

In the previous chapter, I mentioned that builders who are serious about what they do often see themselves constructing not just houses, but legacies for the future. Building houses represents their way of making a difference in the world. They meet and help fulfill a basic desire—some would say a basic right—of Americans to own their own homes. You're here to support that dream.

Here's a challenge: Describe what you do in 16 seconds. Here are some examples:

"I supply high quality, framing and trim products that allow the builder to construct a more affordable home."

"I consult with builders on computer services that will make them more efficient in tracking costs."

"I find prospective homeowners and help their dreams come true by matching their ability to pay with the proper builder."

"My skill as finish carpenter gives the crowning touch to all efforts by the builder to make the house look its best before closing."

Get the picture? You don't supply windows and doors, you supply products that add long-term value and design to the house with their ease of cleaning and maintenance. You don't supply appliances; you ship and service products that provide the ultimate in versatility and convenience in the kitchen. You don't sell accounting services, you offer reliable information in a confidential manner that will ensure the builder has an accurate recording of his or her business financial information. Again, what do you really do? Write that 16-second description of what you do one more time.

This statement should say what you really do. Repeat it until it feels as natural to say as the name of your company. Think about how you get up in the morning, about what keeps you doing what you need to do when others would have become discouraged and quit or directed their energies elsewhere. I refer to this inner drive as purpose. Your purpose for a particular year reflects your past. Consider major events from the past year. How have they helped shape the person you are today? When you were not successful, what did you learn that strengthened your value to your company and to the building community?

A fortunate few have yet another factor shaping how they sell to builders. They have a mentor, one with valuable experience in life and business. A colleague would make an excellent mentor, someone they could observe and learn from, even from that person's mistakes. Mentors can be builders or associates. I was fortunate to observe several people during my early years of selling to builders. When asked, they provided advice or counsel, made introductions, or just listened. If you do not have a mentor or have not benefited from such a relationship, it may not be too late to find one. Or, consider becoming one to the next generation. Think about all the lessons you have learned. What a valuable contribution you could make to the future of the housing industry by sharing your insights with those who will follow in your footsteps.

Whether you are in the beginning stages of your career or have been around a while, take time over the next day or so to think about your purpose in selling to builders. For example, a trim carpenter might write, "In this year, my purpose will be to bring a high quality of workmanship and attention to the details of my craft that will separate me from those who are in the same trade. I will not let the pressure of time and competition keep me from producing the finest trim work in my market."

Once you've composed your statement, carry it with you and review it often. This statement will help you stay focused while your competition is distracted. You play an important part in giving shape to the great American dream of homeownership: You are helping to turn dreams into reality for more than a million families each year.

You have already begun an effective plan for selling to builders: You have a basic appreciation for your strengths and know which skills need work. And you've put together a plan to develop both. Your personal mission statement partially reflects that inward drive, but how do you get the actual sale?

At one time supply companies took new salespeople, gave them a catalogue of what was available, and said, "Go get 'em." A trade contractor might grow tired of working for someone else and decide to go into business and deal directly with builders. At that time both just went out and started calling on builders. While some were successful, many were not. Often the salesperson and trade contractor simply assumed they knew what each builder wanted, and they often wound up feeling frustrated. That need not be the case with you. This book can help you find and maintain that focus on the builder.

When Do You Do What You Do?

The time tracker in Figure 2.4 is designed to help you see how you spend your business day. Use 15-minute segments over a 30-day period to track where you spend your time. At times it may seem like a nuisance to use, but you'll find the results gratifying: You will clearly see just how you spend your days.

Modify the form's layout to fit what you do. As you progress during the month, take time to review results every two weeks during your planning session. Be ready for some surprises. After you see where you spend your time during an entire month, modify next month's schedule to devote more time to what you are paid to do—sell to builders. If activities are distracting your sales efforts and you answer to someone in management, share the results with them. They may be able to use this information to get you some assistance in dealing with issues that prevent you from selling.

Trade contractors must use the form a little differently, since much of their day is spent on a single job. If that's the case, figure out how much time you spend contacting potential builders in the immediate area. Contact other builders in the development where you are working by inviting them to visit a job that's underway. You might use a postcard mailer to tell builders what you are doing and invite them to come by. Ask the builder for whom you are currently working if you can place your sign out front. Take pictures of work as it progresses. Different builders like to be contacted at different times of day. Successful trade contractors and suppliers who are part of your network will let you know the best time to call. Follow-up calls to builders come early in the morning (before 8 am) or in the early evening—before 7 pm.

Goal Setting

Purpose is just a grand idea without goals to set into play. Purpose-based goals can transform your level of success in short order. Do you have goals related to selling to builders? Have you committed them to writing? Do you review them daily? If you cannot answer all three in the affirmative, read on and follow the directions. Your business will begin to expand immediately.

The principles of effective goal setting are simple. When applied, they maximize your time and energy in selling to builders. Let's assume today begins a new year. A new calendar graces your wall, pocket, or purse as well as the banner of your local newspaper. You have already crossed out the old year and 365 brand new days are looking you in the eye. They represent 365 opportunities to do what you have always wanted to do. Filled with resolve? Here you go.

FIGURE 2.4 Time Tracker

Date _____

Time	Travel	Sales Call	Pros-pecting	Cust. Service	P.R.	Quotes	Product Service	Network	Admin.	Other
07:15										
07:30										
07:45										
08:00										
08:15										
08:30										
08:45										
09:00										
09:15										
09:30										
09:45										
10:00										
10:15										
10:30										
10:45										
11:00										
11:15										
11:30										
11:45										
12:00										
12:15										
12:30										
12:45										
01:00										
01:15										
01:30										
01:45										
02:00										
02:15										
02:30										
02:45										
03:00										
03:15										
03:30										
03:45										
04:00										
04:15										
04:30										
04:45										
05:00										

Goal setting remains the same regardless of what you do. Most of us choose to live within the walls of our potential, rarely venturing outside for a look at the exciting world that awaits those who dare to be more than they are. By nature of the demands of sales or service, you have within you the fire that can lead to extraordinary achievement. Go beyond the boundaries that seem to encircle you.

As a trade contractor, you may long to express your skills and talents in a manner that makes you and what you do stand out from the competition. As a salesperson for a supplier to builders, you may be driven by a need to be recognized as an authority in your field. If you are in a service-related industry, you may choose to be known as a firm that sets the standard for what you do.

You need a basis for goal setting. Combine vision and purpose to go beyond where you are and beyond the expected. Do that, and your dreams will begin to leave your head and heart and take on the shape of reality.

Before beginning, you must know the following:

- What do you want to accomplish?
- When do you want it to happen?
- What do you need to make it happen?
- Why do you want to do it?

Armed with this information, you can begin to formulate your goals and commit them to writing.

Four Simple Principles of Goal Setting

Follow these four principles when setting your goals, and you will maximize your chances for success:

- Make your goals specific.
- List your goals in order of importance.
- Assign a reasonable time frame to accomplish each goal.
- Develop a way to measure each goal.

Make Your Goals Specific. It would be easy to write, "In this new year, I am going to sell more lumber." But what exactly does "more" mean? Three more job lots, six more truckloads, an additional $500,000 in sales? Give yourself precise information with which to direct your efforts. Make up your list, and address the second principle.

List Your Goals in Order of Importance. Ranking your goals can be tough but critical. Which ones are the most important? Then, when you need to be in three places at once, you can more easily choose exactly where you need to go or what you need to do.

The end result of all these steps is a person who knows how to maximize time, and salespeople and trade contractors consider time a precious commodity. Setting goals will also help you focus your attention and energy, and help you stop "chasing rabbits"—tending to tasks that distract you from your urgent goals.

Assign a Reasonable Time Frame to Accomplish Each Goal. In recent years, as I deliver workshops to groups with several generations present, I have learned that reasonable time is relative. An increasing number of people in our culture want what they want, now. They cannot wait.

But good things, fulfilling things, are worth waiting for. Give yourself some room. With multiple responsibilities at work, at home, and in the community, you can easily get into trouble when you try to get everything done at once. Give yourself some slack. Divide your goals into short- (one year), medium- (three to five years), and long-term categories. You are in charge of this system; let it work for you. Set a time to get the job done, and begin to plan toward that date.

Try the time chart for goals in Figure 2.5. The chart allows you to track progress on a daily, semi-weekly, and weekly basis. It may also help you develop the discipline needed to see those medium- and long-term goals through to fulfillment. By making daily notations of what you accomplished toward your goals, you stay on task. Time, circumstances, and the clutter of tiny daily tasks have less chance to sneak up on you. You have your goals, specifically stated, reasonable in scope and in priority.

Develop a Way to Measure Each Goal. The last principle in the chain is measurement. Whether you use a chart, timeline, or some other device, measuring progress toward your goal reinforces your efforts. Let your imagination come up with a means of charting your steps to completion.

With everything in place, put your plan in action. Place your goals on 3 × 5 index cards; carry one in your pocket calendar, post one on your bathroom mirror, or stick one on the dash of your vehicle. Want to be a little more creative? Make your reminders memorable: use construction paper, cut them in odd shapes. Or, take a cue from the *Making Your Membership Work* exercise in NAHB's Profit By Association Workshop[2] and place your goals not in words, but in symbols. How you get there doesn't matter, so long as you're recording and reviewing daily.

It also doesn't matter exactly where you put your reminders, just be able to see them and review them each day. Some people prefer to do this at the end of the day as they're planning for tomorrow. Note accomplishments, show progress toward your goals, and get ready for the next challenge. If a stumbling block appears, take time to plan around it. Visualize yourself getting the sale, converting the customer, making the first delivery, or cashing the first check.

If you have a particularly challenging goal, don't be put off by negative reactions from people with whom you share your quest. Cut out negative influences as best you can; a daily dose of reinforcement from positive people will help feed you. Surround yourself with others who are growing and positive, perhaps even working toward the same goal. It may serve to encourage you and the others in the whole process.

Most goals are of sufficient size that reaching them will demand much time and effort. Let your successes toward achieving those goals keep you enthusiastic and involved. Seeing yourself in a better light will not only build your confidence, this newfound confidence will strengthen you to face any roadblocks that may appear in your quest to sell to builders.

But all the preparation of pondering, recording, and reviewing will not take on their hidden powers until you actually carry out your goals.

FIGURE 2.5 Time Chart for Goals

Day	One Year	Three Year	Five Year
1			
2			
3			
4			
5			
6			
7			
8			
9			
10			
11			

My One Year Goal is: My Three Year Goal is: My Five Year Goal is:

_____   _____   _____

_____   _____   _____

_____   _____   _____

3

Build a Plan
of Action

How do you shape a plan that reflects your capabilities, your assortment of products and/or services, and bring all these elements together to meet the needs of the builder?

How big or grand should it be? Now is not the time to be timid; be bold. If you are a sole proprietor in sales or service or if you work for a larger company that has no formal sales planning format, the Personal Sales Planner (Figure 3.1) will help you outline your market goals for the coming year. As you fill in the blanks, you will see just how little of your time you actually spend selling. Why do salespeople spend so little time doing what they are paid to do?

Lack of Focus. The biggest reason for not spending more time in front of the builder is a lack of focus on what is most important for a particular period of the day. If you sell products or services to builders, you've probably had days or weeks when what you really needed to do was swallowed up by seemingly more urgent needs from other builders, usually across town from where you planned to be. The Personal Sales Planner will help you stay focused.

Travel Time. Another impediment to spending profitable selling time in front of the builder is the time spent traveling from location to location. Cellular telephones ease the strain, but you are still more efficient selling face-to-face. The Personal Sales Planner offers a simple form to help you determine where to spend your time. You determine how long to use it, but to get accurate results you'll need to use it for at least a complete rotation of your sales area. Again, one of the chief benefits will be the realization of how much time you actually spend selling. While you can't neglect customer service, travel, telephone follow-up, or paperwork, your real money and builder impact will come by selling the full range of goods and services you offer.

A Guide to the Personal Sales Planner

The Personal Sales Planner is divided into three parts. No matter whether you are a salesperson or own a company that sells to your entire region, you need to look for the total market picture. The first part of the planner shows you where your business stands. The second part helps you decide where it needs to go. Section III looks at how you can promote builder business (Figure 3.1).

Section I.A.—Sales history examines your current business' sales volume and location. Begin by tracing the number of local housing starts, information that should be available through your local home builders association. Track the last four years and check to see if you can obtain a forecast for the coming year. These figures are for single-family, both detached and attached, and multifamily units. You may even have

---

FIGURE 3.1 The Personal Sales Planner

NAME_____ LOCATION_____

I. WHERE YOU HAVE BEEN?

A. Sales history: **Housing start history (if available)**

200__   200__   200__   200__

200__   200__   200__   200__

(Some companies measure market share by establishing a ratio of average sale of their product line or service to the number of housing units produced during the calendar year. The use of this type of ratio is not perfect but affords an indicator of where you are in estimating your share of the overall market.)

B. Sales by customer: 80/20 rule

	Name	Location(s)	Sales	Key service or product lines	% to total
1.					
2.					
3.					
4.					
5.					
6.					
7.					
8.					
9.					
10.					
11.					
12.					

FIGURE 3.1 The Personal Sales Planner (*Continued*)

C. Major geographic areas

Zone	Customer Name	Sales	% to total—Customers	% to total—Sales	Frequency
1.					
2.					
3.					
4.					
5.					

(How is your territory shaped? NSEW of a particular part of a central city, or by town, section of city? Most sales areas have either natural or manmade boundaries.)

D. List major products or services by customer and territory.

Zone	Area	Product sales or service	Type	% to total	GP generated
1.					
2.					
3.					
4.					
5.					

(Some areas, because of builder make-up, have one type of product or service you supply or install versus another. You can have mixed categories in a single sales zone.)

Multifamily(MF)　　　　Light Commercial(LC)
Single family-Detached(SF-D)　　Remodelers(REM)
Single family-Attached(SF-A)　　Combination(Combo)

E. Your use of time

List by percentage of your work week.

☐ Sales calls on established builders
☐ Sales calls on prospective builders
☐ Service of the product
☐ Installation of the product
☐ Customer service
☐ Travel
☐ Home Builder's Association meetings/events
☐ Administrative: paperwork/reports/quotes
☐ Networking
☐ Sales meetings

FIGURE 3.1 The Personal Sales Planner (*Continued*)

F. Product or service offerings

Products or services	2001	2002	2003
A. _____	☐	☐	☐
B _____	☐	☐	☐
C. _____	☐	☐	☐
D. _____	☐	☐	☐
E. _____	☐	☐	☐

II. WHERE ARE YOU GOING?

A. What is your sales goal? Dollar volume, % of increase, number of new accounts, % of market share, etc. Be specific. _____

_____

B. Projected sales by key accounts and territories

	Name	Location	Sales of major product/service	% to total
1.				
2.				
3.				
4.				
5.				
6.				
7.				
8.				
9.				
10.				
11.				
12.				

C. What is your new account goal? _____

D. Top ten prospects

	Name	Type	Current source/supplier	Location	Potential volume
1.					
Key to success					
2.					
Key to success					
3.					
Key to success					
4.					
Key to success					

FIGURE 3.1 The Personal Sales Planner (*Continued*)

D. Top ten prospects (*continued*)

	Name	Type	Current source/supplier	Location	Potential volume
5.					
Key to success					
6.					
Key to success					
7.					
Key to success					
8.					
Key to success					
9.					
Key to success					
10.					

This information will be transferred to the Potential Builder form for follow-through.

III. SALES PROMOTION

A. Home Builder's Association involvement

Association	Event	Date	Cost

B. Other promotions

Item	Purpose	# Needed	Cost

someone in your market who can project what will occur in remodeling; place your sales figures in that same ballpark.

If you are looking for a ratio to plot your share of the market, simply figure the average sale per home for your product and/or service and divide it by the number of starts. If, for example, you sell roofing and the average new house in your market takes 25 squares, then multiply the number of starts times 25 to get the total market. Follow the total market figure with the number of squares sold, and that gives you your share of the market.

Next, create a profile of your customer base. The Personal Sales Planner allows you to see what you want done by market segment. Where have you spent your time? Has working with those segments been profitable? Was that profit sufficient for the time and energy expended? What segments of the market could increase with more of your attention?

Current Builder Base Profile

Section I.B—In Sales by Customer, list builders by location first. Each sales territory has certain defined geographic boundaries. What are yours? Place your customer base in the appropriate area. Rank builders by gross sales and percentage of gross profits. This ranking will give you a specific guide to who is doing what, how much, and where. Any surprises?

Reconfigure your time during the next selling season so you can spend more time visiting the people who have been the most profitable for you. What can you do to enhance your position with them? How can you encourage builders whose sales dropped in the past year?

Next classify builders by type of construction: single or multifamily, light commercial, and the like by sales volume. Use the Classification codes in Section I.D (List major products or services by customer and territory) of the Personal Sales Planner to speed up the process.

How often do you see these customers? How often should you see them? Consistent contact keeps the competition at bay while allowing you to learn about, and then anticipate, emerging needs. Which products or services sold best and produced the best return? Should you change your offerings for the New Year or perhaps enhance an overall product line to make it even stronger?

Section I.C—Major geographic areas allows you to review how you've spent your time. Any surprises here? Look where most of the builders you sell to or service are located and compare that with where you have spent your time. That comparison can allow you to define your approach to the overall market and simply be more efficient.

Section I.F—Product or service offerings addresses what you sell. List your core products or services by gross sales using a three-year model, if possible. If you are new to the territory, your sales manager can provide this information. Rank these products or services by gross profit.

This process may seem like overkill, but at the end you can look at a single page that lists what most of your customers buy and at what margin. Any hints as to what you'll need to add sales or profit? This may seem like sales manager stuff, but some salespeople do both sales and sales management. You are in charge of your territory. If it doesn't produce, who is responsible?

All your work begins to take serious shape as you head into Section II (Where are you going?). Begin by writing specific goals for yourself.

Choosing New Products

Section II.B—You will find **Projected sales by key accounts and territories** offers more challenges. You'll need to rate these products or services by the time needed to sell and service them. Are you finding items that demand a great deal of time but provide little return? Look for the 80-20 ratio (Section I.B). The 80-20 rule says you will lose, on average, 20 percent of your base every year. According to author and speaker Brian Tracy, this rule was developed in 1895 by Vil Fredo Pareto, an Italian economist, who suggested most societies could be divided into the "Vital Few" (20 percent) and the "Trivial Many" (80 percent). The theory, which holds true in study after study, is that 20 percent of the people, products, customers, prospects, etc. account for 80 percent of the value.

Always listen proactively for needs that arise from a builder. What products or services could you add to replace those that have been drains on your time and profit? New products and services give you a great excuse for a substantive sales call and can compel a builder to take time away from the company's current project to look, listen, and comment. A new product or service could separate you from the competition. How will you choose that product?

You can discover a great deal about your industry by regularly reading housing-related periodicals. Look for ideas among their displays of new products for builders. You may see something that fills a need you've heard expressed by a builder.

Before adding a product, though, check out whether it's been well received. Ask for a list of suppliers from the vendor, then contact them and listen to what they have to say. No matter how great the product or advertising may appear to be, if the manufacturer cannot deliver it to you in a timely fashion on a consistent basis, the product is not worth pursuing. Remember that time can work against a builder; your goal is to help.

If you are considering a commodity product such as lumber, drywall, or roofing material, determine whether the vendor has a price and a strong commitment to service that will enable you to satisfy this demanding market.

What kind of brand recognition does the manufacturer carry? This issue is best decided on a local basis. Builders often prefer locally or regionally produced products, so not all nationally advertised brand names carry strong recognition into every local market. What kind of reputation do the national products hold in your market? If the national company already has some local presence, why are the manufacturers looking for more distribution in your area?

If you know little about the company or the product, determine what kind of commitment the manufacturer will make to you as one of its suppliers or distributors. Some important questions to ask the manufacturer are:

- How much worker-power are the manufacturers willing to expend to help you build brand or product awareness?
- What kind of advertising (money and material) is available for that effort?
- What kind of inventory do you or the builder need, and are the manufacturers willing to extend terms until the product has received sufficient exposure?

As you look at your offerings, you will probably discover a product or service that has been or is demanding much time and capital to keep it in the market—at the expense of other lines. You may have a key account or two that uses that line, so don't drop it, but make sure you note this fact when you evaluate the best use of your time and products.

Growth Plans

Section II.B—Projected sales by key accounts and territories of the Personal Sales Planner is the heart of your growth plans for the coming year: the addition of new accounts. In Chapter 8 you'll create a network of people and organizations to feed you with the leads you'll need for continuous growth. If you have been in the business any length of time, you have experienced the comings and goings of builders from your customer base. If the 80-20 rule holds true (and your past sales records can tell you your retention rate), you will need a 40 percent increase in new accounts to see a 20 percent gain in accounts overall.

This Personal Sales Planner limits you to the top 10 accounts you plan to add in the new selling season. You will have more; expand this form to any number you wish. Your current closing rate will help you determine how many target accounts you'll need to meet your goal. Your closing rate will help you plan how many letters, follow-up calls, and face-to-face sales calls are needed to reach your target.

This tight list of 10 identifies for you and those you report to (if you do) which accounts will receive extra attention from you. And it details what you need to do to win them over from the competition. What does your company need to do to support your efforts in obtaining this vital new business? Be specific.

When you look for builders to add to your top 10, ask the following questions:

- How much do I know about how they do business?
- What do we need to do to service the account when we are successful?
- What terms are they looking for?
- What products are they currently buying?
- What kind of reputation do they have on the street?
- Do they have good credit?
- If I added a manufacturer's product line or service, would I have a story to tell the next prospect?

Section I.E—Your use of time of the Personal Sales Planner will provide great insight into how you spend your time. Change compels you to keep adding to your builder base, and you do that by increasing the number of prospects you see on a regular basis. This basic list allows you to come to terms with nonselling functions that drain your time and energy and produce nothing in sales. You spend the most profitable part of your day with builders. The exercise in Figure 2.5 will help you increase that amount of time.

Section I.F—Product or service offerings gives you a place to record the products or services that drive your business. List your five main categories and sales for the last three years. Then place the gross profit figure beside each year. Do any trends appear? Any surprises?

Section II.A—What is your sales goal? and Section II.C—What is your new account goal?. Record your sales goal in Section II.A in dollars or units or whichever way you choose to list it. Using the guidelines from Chapter 2, write out effective goals in specific, accountable, and measurable statements.

Section II.B—Projected sales by key accounts and territories appraises the impact a new year has on your current accounts. What do you expect these builders to do in the next selling season? Do you see any shifts coming? Has last year's ranking changed? Do the new rankings indicate a shift in size or location or in what you are selling? What can you sell more of from your current product line?

What new service or product can you add to your selling strategy to increase your sales to these trusted, long-term customers?

Section II.C—What is your account goal? This section provides a place for you to state your account goal for this new selling season. A simple question, but you need to make a sufficient number of calls to prospective builders to make it happen. So what is your closing ratio? How do you find that number? There are no hard statistics on closing ratios available for most of the businesses that serve builders, so you must rely on personal experience, company standards, or the experience of members of your network. Here is a basic approach.

Simply put, how many sales calls do you have to make before a prospective builder says yes? Calls are defined as the various manners you use to contact the prospect. How many telephone, fax, mail, e-mail, or in-person contacts do you have to make on a daily basis for that to happen? Whatever the figure, include it in your plans. If the ratio is one in 10, and you have no established basis to judge your performance, you need ____ calls to stay even, and ____ to cover the increase and meet your sales goal. You fill in the blanks; your results will depend on what part of the supply or trade contractor portion of the business you are in and what level of volume you need to produce to stay profitable.

Part of the planning process for a new business requires you to answer some tough questions about yourself and your company:

- Do you really want to sell to every builder, or do you have certain criteria they must meet?
- Does their sales volume, number of units, or location determine how well you can service them once they have said yes?
- Some products require more follow-through once they are sold or installed than others do. Is the builder strong enough financially to pay on time so you can sell or install and still remain profitable?
- Will you be able to sell at a sufficient markup to support the product once it is shipped?

Knowing this basic information will save you time, allowing you to approach only those builders who fit your target profile. You cannot sell everyone, but you need to sell everyone you can and everything you can.

Section II.D—Top 10 Prospects lists your top 10 prospects based on the 80-20 rule. This list will be part of your new account goal. Where are the 10 located? What do they buy that you offer? Would they benefit from an expanded offering of products or services? Who is your competition and what will they do to counter your advances on their customers? Make sure you know the key items these prospects want. Compiling this information puts in one place the facts you and/or your company must know to secure these vital new builders as customers.

Recalling from personal and sometimes painful experience, you will see a plus-or-minus 20 personal loss of current business from this year to the next. If you are planning on a real increase, it will have to come from potential builders plus increased sales to current customers. These accounts will go into your weekly sales call rotation.

Get the Builder Involved

How do you get all this valuable information on paper? Involve your builder customer base in the planning process and you'll reap the rewards. The more basic the information, the more valuable it will be. Practice the three R's of selling to builders: Research, Reviewing information, and Response.

Research. When was the last time you sat down with your key customers and discussed how you are performing for them? A key customer is sensitive to the marketplace and its forces, adjusting to meet the demands of the present while planning for the future. You identified these people in Chapter 3. Ask what they think about your company and its offering. Which of their suggestions would lead to greater customer service or a new product offering?

The numbers that you record have more validity when they lose the wistfulness of your optimism and gain the grit of the builder's perspective. You get that information by using proactive listening techniques.

Reviewing Information. Reviewing that information and gathering more comprises the second "R." Listening should be as natural as breathing or talking. (My dad was fond of saying that people were born with two ears and one mouth and should use them proportionally.)

Most people need a short course in proactive listening. A myth that salespeople need to overcome is the archetypal impression that a real salesperson keeps talking until the sale comes through. More often, a salesperson can actually lose a sale by droning on long after the presentation has been made, literally talking himself or herself out of the deal. Proactive listening is a technique that requires the use of open-ended questions, ones that require more than a yes or no answer.

"Gee, aren't we having great weather?" is a closed question, while "What kind of impact has our weather had on your business lately?" is an open-ended one. They look for the same basic information but allow a variety of possibilities in answering.

Proactive listening often adds value to conversation. It involves restating the content of the speaker's statement, and providing clarification and understanding. Proactive listening encourages the speaker to elaborate: "Did I understand you to say... ?"

When you employ this type of listening you learn about real needs, which can point you to your customer's goals. Listening for needs has given birth to next-day package delivery, one-hour dry-cleaning or photo-processing, energy-efficient building products, and of course, the drive-through at your favorite fast-food restaurant. Listening gives you a great opening to an added service.

- "What can I do to help you sell more houses?"
- "What can I do to help you finish five days closer to budget?"
- "What can we do to help you decrease the number of call backs?"
- "How can we help you eliminate much of your lumber shrinkage?"

Can you provide a new product or service? If not, maybe you'll think of an additional need for your service/product line. Or, ask members of your network for suggestions that will help the builder meet his or her goal. If you provide a referral, everyone wins.

Response. The third "R" of selling to builders is response. Using proactive listening techniques demonstrates that you have heard what has been said and can draft an agreement that reflects the expectations between you and the builder. These suggestions are your solutions to the builder's dilemmas. Depending on when you or your company begins the planning process for next year, you can record these mutual expectations and, if needed, record both signatures. If your industry does not have such a form, use the one in Figure 3.2.

Use this simple form for a year to give you information to share with builders when you discuss the year's progress. By doing so you reduce the number of calls that have no purpose other than to discuss the latest ball score or weather. This Partnership Agreement will contain a target sales goal that can be easily tracked by recording monthly progress in a Customer Management File (Figure 7.1). Listening and responding are hallmarks of a customer-centered company. You and your company will find that the road to success will not be crowded when you choose to go the extra mile.

What you learn by listening to the builder can provide an excellent opportunity for you or your marketing resource people to counsel the builder or his or her sales staff or real estate agents. What can you do to help him or her sell more houses?

The agreement also allows you to put in writing those characteristics that separate you from your competition. Specify "hot buttons" you know are important to the builder. Put a copy in the builder's file, and if you have a sales support staff, make them aware of the builder's needs and keep a copy handy. Suggest to the staff or the builder that your competition does not or cannot do the job in the same manner that you can. If you are a tradesperson, emphasize these distinctions.

Use one or more of the following:

- Jobsite cleaned daily with debris put in the bin.
- Returns and credits issued with seven days of receipt.
- Service requests filled within 48 hours.
- Keys placed in the proper box by the crew before leaving the job.

You may already be doing these tasks, but when they are placed in front of the builder in writing, they take on a greater emphasis and set you apart from your com-

FIGURE 3.2 Partnership Agreement

The builder agrees to...	The trade contractor/supplier agrees to...
Build 25 houses this year	Provide paint and wallpaper per quote
Give 10-day lead time with colors	Give 45 days notice on price change
Pay 10 days from invoice	
Give 48 hours notice on call-backs	Take care of call-backs within 48 hours

petition. Builders are a major source of information about market projections for the upcoming year. Add input from trusted members of your network as well as future-savvy developers and real estate agents. Some standard databases also show these trends. These sources can help you judge the potential size of your local market in the coming year.

You still must decide what facets of the housing market you want to focus on:

Single or multifamily? Attached or detached? Semi-custom or custom? Each segment has its own character and needs. Is your company large enough to meet them all?

Even when you put the Personal Sales Planner into action, you will need to stay abreast not only of your customers and how they are progressing through the year, but also of trends that will impact the building industry.

Other Sources of Information

General membership meetings of your local home builders association provide an opportunity to share information with builders and associates alike. And a cross section of members generally allows you to confirm or deny information. These meetings provide a great opportunity to network as well, but don't do only hard selling; builders say they want to enjoy themselves.

Many local home builders associations and all state associations produce a newsletter or magazine on a regular basis. Read it. If an active legislative effort is underway in your town or state, the newsletter will carry an article about it, usually written by your contact person. What happens at the local courthouse, city council, and state house directly impacts housing. Stay in touch.

Review the monthly issues of *Builder* and *Professional Builder* magazines. These fine publications provide great data and track trends. Whether this information involves the mood in Washington, fluctuations in interest rates, or the price of framing lumber, it will affect your sales to builders. The housing industry is national in scope; the more informed you are on issues from all jurisdictions, the better prepared you are to meet builders' changing needs. You need an abundance of accurate, substantive information when you make a sales call.

While each locale differs, many newspapers offer business-savvy columns that address local issues. And locally focused business magazines abound. These can help you keep in touch with the broader business climate in your area. Remember, the building industry is not isolated. It reflects the general mood of the community, one part of a diverse economic tapestry. This intertwining of what may appear to be diverse business interests may impact the housing industry (your chief concern) negatively or positively.

Home builders associations bring to their members an invaluable tracking of political issues that involve the industry. Avail yourself of such information. One of the concepts it took years for me to appreciate was the size of the home building industry in local terms. Take your local home builders association membership and multiply the number of builders and the number of associate firms by the average number of employees. That will give you an appreciation for the number of jobs that depend on responsible growth in your market.

With that figure in mind, please remember that groups in many areas want to put you out of business by slowing growth or eliminating it altogether. Don't stop to examine their motivations, but be on notice that they are there. Look for their activity in your area; your job and the jobs of your coworkers may be on the line.

Get the Word Out

Section III of the Personal Sales Planner looks at how your promotional efforts help you maintain and increase your business. You could reasonably budget up to 1 percent of projected sales for promotion. You have two basic avenues to sell people on what you do.

The first is active involvement in your local home builders association and other civic organizations. In addition to dues, you will incur other charges as you support the organization's efforts and promote yourself. What events should you sponsor? That answer will come in part from your response to these questions:

- What positions do you hold or on which committees do you serve as part of the local home builders association?
- How do you measure these items?
- How effectively have you spent your time? Can you justify the time and money you've expended for what you've received?
- What are your plans for next year? Where do you need to spend your time and money to be more effective than last year?

Section III.B—Other promotions addresses the hard dollars you need for your promotional or advertising efforts in the coming year. What are your plans? In which periodicals, newsletters, or membership directories will you advertise and what are the rates? What will you say in the ad (or ads)? Who will design it? What events will you sponsor outside of your association activities? Will you have a fishing trip or a golf outing? How about an open house or cookout? Have you considered incentive trips for builders? Will your company or supplier cosponsor the event?

The most obvious forms of advertising are items such as pamphlets or informational packets, pens, notepads, and such that you give to builders and important employees. What can you deliver to the jobsite or leave with the gatekeeper? What items can you put into their hands that will prove more distinctive than a pen or a calendar? Whatever you do, make it memorable and easy to use. Then every time they use it they'll think of you.

Whom do you treat to meals, play golf with, take fishing, present with gift certificates, or recognize on birthdays and anniversaries? These considerations are part of this activity and need to be budgeted. The more gross profit dollars builders produce for you the more promotional dollars you need to allow for use on them. What kind of support are they looking for in the new year? Are you a source of co-op advertising? Are you allowing your vendors who have these monies available to be part of your annual promotion budget?

As you pull your promotional ideas together, think ahead to those times in the coming sales year when you will need to present the builder with some token of appreciation. The winter holidays are a good example. What are you doing to recognize and thank builders for doing business with you in the past year? Is it something you bought off the shelf at a discount warehouse because the price was right? After all, you need to give them something. Why not take the great information that you know about your customers and their key employees and give them something that will set you apart from the competition.

Putting Your Personal Sales Planner to Work

After a through review of the Personal Sales Planner, you are now ready to implement your plan. Use a map of your territory, and the information and insight gained from this exercise, to locate the principal geographical zones in your territory. Plot the number of customers in each zone, then add a second listing of the number of potential builders in each zone.

How often should you see each one? In mapping your territory you're trying to increase your exposure to current and potential customers. Remember that sellers devote less than 37 percent of the average sales day in actual face-to-face selling. The single biggest drain on your time and energy is driving from location to location. As you plan an average week, consider which zones need more attention and which can be put on less than a daily rotation? Our survey showed that, regardless of their size, 59 percent of the builders looked for the salesperson at least once a week.

Your builder base will tell you how often you need to show up. Ask them, listen, and act accordingly. How many face-to-face calls do you need to make to maintain proper contact with your customer base? How many would prefer telephone contact? The survey I conducted in conjunction with researching this book indicated that 48 percent of builders worked through inside sales contacts. Can those in your company be persuaded to work diligently to keep the lines of communication open between your organization and the builder? How often do you mail out updates of new products and services?

As you pull this information together, keep in mind that you must constantly search out new customers to increase your sales base. As a rule, you'll lose 20 percent of your base each year, so you'll need the same percentage increase just to stay even. Take time to accumulate a list of at least 10 key prospects to start. Where do they build? Size? Price? Reputation? Are they compatible with what you do as a company? Do you know anyone connected with the companies: clerical or site superintendents? Is the company worthy of your time to pursue? Is it credit-worthy? Do you have the products or services they want or need? Can your company meet their reasonable delivery schedules? What is the company's estimated volume or estimated sales dollars per house for those who supply goods and trade?

While pulling this list together, contact members of your network who know the prospect's reputation with other trades and suppliers and service industries. To be successful, you'll need to meet the builder's expectations. If other trade contractors or suppliers are under consideration, see if you can determine why. Rank them by size of potential volume and priority of calling. Will success with these builders offer sufficient sales volume to cover the 80-20 rule?

Merge this list with that from **Section II.D—Top 10 Prospects** of the Personal Sales Planner, and make them part of the mix. How often do you see them? Brian

Tracy suggests in his sales workshops that the following results occur in contacting prospects:

- 50 percent quit after the first contact
- 18 percent quit after the second contact
- 7 percent quit after the third contact
- 5 percent quit after the fourth contact
- 20 percent stay after the fifth contact and eventually get the sale

Persistence produces that fire down below and shows in your eyes and actions. Part of your progress may come when you are told no, for an old adage says that, "Salesmanship begins when the customer says no. Persistence is more than a noble trait; it is the ability to have the potential customer slam the door, kick you out, refuse your calls, ignore your letters, hang up in mid-conversation, and still come back.

I have been privileged to work with and observe strong sales and tradespeople over the years. One who stands out in my mind works as a salesperson in a major Midwestern market in a consistently strong and highly competitive territory. Several years ago I received a call from him one evening. He had been pursuing a certain customer for more than eight years, watching his competition deliver product, eight years of sitting or standing in waiting rooms to pick up plans or deliver quotes, eight years of takeoffs and meetings all ending in no's. Yet, that day the customer said yes. He had found the right button and, now a familiar and trusted face, he closed the sale.

While the sale was not the largest of his remarkable career, it was the principle, and I felt a great satisfaction for him. His experience was an inspiration to his peers and proves that persistence pays on more than one level.

Did he ignore the remainder of his customer base during this time or not call on other prospects? No, he worked in the potential accounts with builders who are already regular purchasers. His success indicates that organization and persistence work well together in keeping sales alive and growing.

Expanding the reach of services and territories remains a challenge that faces those who serve the growing needs of builders. The process is simple. If followed, more sales at more profit will not be far behind.

Opening New Territories

As you add to your customer base, you may choose to open up new territories. If so, keep these thoughts in mind as a basic guide.

Before you begin evaluating the strength of the market, determine whether you and your firm can service the area. If the expansion will stretch your resources to the point of jeopardizing the rest of your business, think carefully. If you deliver your product from a warehouse, be sure to consult with the people who will need to add to inventory, handle and deliver existing equipment, and maintain a reasonable delivery schedule in the proposed territory.

Once you've answered those questions positively, research the strength of the market. A number of services companies have kept track of housing starts by counties, cities, or villages. If you know a developer or a member of your network who has contacts in the new area, consult them. Also talk with a savvy real estate agent who knows the industry in this new territory.

If the prospective territory has a professional builders association, spend some time with the executive officer. I have found over the years that these people generally have a great knowledge of their local market and are willing to share the information.

As part of your exploration, translate the information you receive onto a map. Take sufficient time to visit builders and maybe even do some mystery shopping. Find out who is selling what to whom.

By this time you will have developed a list of prospective builders. Do the first of two mailings introducing yourself and your company. Make sure you send something of value in the package so it won't get tossed with the other unsolicited material that floods the average builder.

Call the prospect within three days of receipt of the mail to gauge initial interest. If you have done your homework, you should have identified a product or service that is not already available in the area. Tell the builder what you can do to meet his or her needs.

Once you determine the strength of the territory and have some prospective builders to see, you will want to schedule at least 20 percent of the next several weeks to travel and develop the territory. You might travel with a noncompeting member of your network who is currently working the territory. An introduction is a powerful tool. Once you have at least one customer in the territory, you can begin to work it in with your regular rotation.

Plan on spending two to three days in succession in the new area at the beginning. By doing so, you take some of the pressure off the missed call, the "be back tomorrow" routine or, in the case of a hot contact, allow sufficient time to build on the initial relationship. You have also removed the pressure of compressed time from your schedule and can concentrate on the business at hand. A factory representative can add to the flavor of the call. Follow this two- to three-day blitz with two similar days the following week.

Chapter 7 is devoted to assisting you in solid territory management. You now have a plan to go with the goals you have established. Good selling.

4

Help Build Your Company for the Future

Assuming that you are part of a business of more than one person, how well do you know your company? How long have you been an employee? In Chapter 2, I encouraged you to create a personal mission statement and let your goals reflect it. Do you know your company's mission statement?

Do your business goals reflect your company's? An old adage from business school says, "Businesses planned for service are apt to succeed; businesses planned for profit are apt to fail." How long has your company been in the business of meeting the building community's needs?

Age and stability are strong assets when fending off the competition. Where does your company want to be in five years? Where do you fit into the plan? Is the company expanding territories? Adding branches? Is it offering a more diverse array of goods and services? How does your company stack up against the top five competitors in your market for sales volume, trucks, services offered, and employees?

Sales Support Staff

The strength of your company lies in its people. Do a superb job of representing your company and what it offers, and over time you may succeed and get the sale. But if the order is mishandled, lost, ignored, or abused in the delivery process, all the energy you put into building a relationship with the builder is lost.

As a trade contractor, how well do you know your fellow employees? Gauge employee attitudes when they arrive for work and listen to how they answer the telephone. Do you feel good when you call in and hear a live voice on the other end? Can a builder conveniently contact your company? Do you provide 800 numbers when needed? Do you have enough incoming lines to handle heavy call volumes? How long should the average builder have to wait on hold?

What attitude prevails if a problem arises over a sale? Many large companies follow a standard procedure. What is yours? One retailer known for its impeccable service devotes its customer service manual to its employees, directing them to always use their best judgement.

How often and in what manner do you and your company say thank you to a builder? Something nice during the holidays is always appreciated, but what about the rest of the year? Is "thank you" a standard phrase at the end of everyone's calls or whenever a transaction takes place? Early on in life you were taught that "please" and "thank you" are the magic words. They still are.

Are there specific people in place to handle credit, delivery, back orders, telephone orders, and special orders? If not, take a good look at your company's organization. Suggest ways you can meet builders' diverse needs.

How are situations handled when you're unavailable for consultation? A company is only as strong as the person who represents it on the other end of the telephone or behind the wheel of a service or delivery truck. If those people lack the skills to handle difficult questions on a continuing basis, they need to be educated.

Educating Employees

How often does your company offer training to develop customer service or communication skills and educate its employees about your products and/or services? If the answer is never, you're missing a great opportunity to share timely information and insights with fellow employees. A well-educated sales team makes all the difference.

Who educates your company? Is the content sales or product? When builders call about products that operate or need to be installed, do the people they talk to have field knowledge of the product? More and more people skilled in the construction industry can meet those education needs.

The building industry in the United States resembles an international melting pot. You need to communicate with the staff and trade contractors who work for the builders, and so do the members of your sales support team. Your employees who have direct contact with non-English speaking tradespeople need a basic understanding of their language and culture. Invite your sales support staff to join other members of your professional builders association in attending language and/or cultural classes.

Does the management staff of your company spend enough time in the field to grasp what the real world is like outside the office? Give employees more interactions with customers and watch their perspectives change and new ideas emerge.

Does your sales support team know just how timely your company's materials are? Certain materials are more sensitive to abuse once installed, applied, or laid. The chart in Figure 4.1 offers a simple guide for you to share with coworkers.

The items in the products or services column in Figure 4.1 are critical to the continuing construction process and cannot arrive late. Delays, for whatever reason, cost the builder both time and money. The second column lists products that do not hold up well to abuse on the job. If you supply these items or items related to them, be ready to deliver them to the builder near closing.

You can have an enormous impact on those who support you inside the company. Your attitude toward staff members, the builder, and life itself can influence the whole

---

FIGURE 4.1   Critical Needs Schedule

☐ Products or Services	☐ Service-Sensitive Products
☐ Concrete (if slab)	☐ Floors—carpet, vinyl
☐ Framing package	☐ Bath fixtures
☐ Roofing and felt	☐ Tile
☐ Windows/interior doors	☐ Exterior doors (particularly steel)
	Cabinets and vanities
	Drywall

---

team to a great degree. Those staff members who stay in the office or yard may consider your life in outside sales glamorous, even though you know better. Learn their names, including nicknames—and be sure they like those nicknames before you use them. Get to know about their families and what they consider important. Recognize their special days during the year. Birthdays or company anniversaries are good times to drop a card with a word of appreciation for what they do to support you.

When you hear a good word from a builder about the job a fellow employee has done on a particular project or site, take time to contact his or her superior and pass on the good word. People are often quick to pass along criticism, so why not point out those times when people exceed expectations? Good news travels fast. Be upbeat and positive.

Enthusiasm is contagious. Does your inside sales support staff have experience in installing the product they are selling? If not, have them spend time with crews in the field learning the challenges builders and their trade contractors face every day.

Such experiences affect perspective. Encourage a ride-along program so office staff can get out in the field to meet the builders. You'll find this program most valuable for people who handle customer service and/or work in the warehouse. It puts a face with the voice that calls and helps you build lasting relationships with builders.

Communication

To keep your builder business on the increase, keep strong lines of communication open with your sales support team. More than half of all problems in business stem from poor communication. Put in writing actions that are prone to error: orders, service requests, follow-through requests to deal with lost orders, or driving directions. Faxes and e-mails make this process easier.

Taking this extra step will greatly decrease the incidence of panicked customers calling to say an order hasn't shown or of lost crews puzzling over directions to a new development. Carbonless forms are an excellent means of passing along all this information. Any document that obligates your company to perform a service or deliver a product belongs in the hands of the responsible party well before the item is needed. Again, this procedure will lessen panicked calls that interrupt the flow of a salesperson's day.

Directions

Your delivery staff may be more visual than auditory in receiving information; if so, put the directions to a job in the form of an easily understood map. Accurate directions ensure a more efficient trip to the jobsite. Someone once told me that oft-quoted baseball manager and sage Yogi Berra said, "When you come to a fork in the road, take one."[3]

Make service calls and deliveries easy for the people who do them. The time saved will reduce stress in the office or warehouse, lessen the number of emergency calls to you, and cut back on untimely deliveries to the builder.

Streamline ways for your sales support staff to stay in touch. If you work with several people in sales support and wear a beeper, have a code in place that lets you know who called and whether the need appears urgent. That information will allow you a swifter response because you can ask for or dial the party directly and save the normal telephone protocol. When you get such a message, call as soon as possible. Strive to return all calls within 90 minutes.

Dressing for Success

When I began in the industry several year ago, the accepted manner of dress for salespeople was a coat and tie. After a few years, my company was the only one that still required this formality. It made me easy to identify when I arrived on a jobsite—I was the only one wearing a coat and tie. I can still remember the shock of coming to my first National Association of Home Builders convention in Houston and meeting our company's number one salesperson in the country wearing cowboy boots and no tie. His attire matched that of his builders.

If you are in outside sales, use what I learned from that experience: Let your attire match that of the builder you are selling to and servicing. In some cases that means a coat and tie; others will accept what is now called business casual. Some builders could care less how you dress as long as you show up and do a good job. Observe those around you. What do they wear when calling on builders? What does the builder wear?

In recent years, I have started carrying an extra set of clothes to work. When faced with a day that might include crawling around a jobsite doing service-related work, I could clean up in time to make a sales presentation to an architect or a purchasing manager of a large builder. A set of coveralls helps greatly when you're faced with this dilemma.

For a woman in outside sales/service, the principle remains the same, with the application that fits your need. When I left field sales for a management position, one of the people who replaced me was a woman. With strong people skills and a good working knowledge of the product, she was soon on jobsites. She told me on a return visit that the biggest change for her was in her shoes. She had worn low-heel pumps with her business suit right out into the muck and mire that makes up many building sites. The builders loved it, and she was a roaring success. She did change her shoes.

For trade contractors, image looms just as important. While you may not have the budget for promotion, you can project a strong image that will help you and your employees overcome some of the myths that exist in the minds of builders and home-owners. Here are ways that trade contractors have worked at changing the image of what they did.

- A small vinyl siding application firm had all members of its crews wear T-shirts with the name of the company on the back. Its trucks were not the newest in town, but they were kept clean and orderly. The company's sign appeared in front of where the job was being performed.
- A trim carpentry crew adds to the organized look by keeping the job clean as they go and by wearing T-shirts with the company name and logo. When the crew hauls material to a job they use covered trailers or a pickup truck with the same name and logo emblazoned on the side.
- A local plumbing contractor puts his crews in clean trucks and well-fitting uniforms. Keeping trucks clean and organized takes time, but the look pays off with repeat business. Builders notice those things.
- A siding crew installs vinyl using cloth gloves and eliminates the usual dirty siding in gables and corners. The builder doesn't have to follow this crew and have the siding power washed. This same crew cleans up after themselves as they go around the house and thus maintains their part of an orderly jobsite. Real estate brokers and agents love to show houses under construction when this crew is present.

Jobsites are often synonymous with blaring music from a variety of sources, resulting in a cacophony of cultures and musical tastes. One finish carpenter I have worked with plays only classical music. He enters at the stage in the construction cycle where he may be practically alone while working on the house. Because he works in large homes and has a great deal of involvement with the homeowner, he greets them with a smile and music. They are often taken back by the music at first and then pleased. His performance matches the music. Trade contractors are in charge of how you are perceived by the builder and the homeowner. A better image often translates into better pay and a more loyal builder base.

Promotion

Be consistent in your message to the builder and his or her client. Take advantage of your slogan, theme, product, or service emphasis and stay with it; it will pay dividends. Step back occasionally and see how effective you have been in your promotional efforts.

Advertising. The local professional builders association's newsletter or journal offers a guaranteed way to reach builders. The advertising costs are usually affordable, and a newsletter or journal effectively ties together all the methods of advertising to builders.

Make your ad stand out. Choose dynamic graphics, clever or humorous copy, and by all means use pictures. People remember pictures.

Builders love to look at pictures. But image comprises more than just what meets the eye. Maximize your exposure to builder members by participating in key events sponsored by the association. You gain personal attention by serving on the planning committee or the event committee; this positive move will prove to be a good use of your time.

Direct mail. Consider running a promotion to coincide with a given event. Create a mailer detailing the importance of the event to the local builders association and encourage builders to participate. Direct mail offers an easy way to make contact with busy builders.

According to those in the business, if you hear back from more than 3 percent of a new list, consider your campaign a success. Do the math and determine if what you are trying to promote can support such an effort. The response percentage increases if you follow up soon after with a telephone call.

Another effective means of assuring better responses to direct mail: Send something of value along with your message. Magnetic business cards, pocket calendars, and the like are inexpensive to mail and useful to the builder.

Regardless of your company's size, achieving success in selling to builders requires a team effort. Reinforce this commitment through respect, communication at all levels, education, and promotion of your business. These worthy areas of concern are addressed by those who want their businesses to continue to expand. True success must be measured over the long-term.

Your investment in affirming those you work with will pay off in the future with great dividends for your business, all the while providing a positive atmosphere in which to work. The attention that you spend in building good communication will pay off as well. Whether getting the word out on a new product to your customer or confirming an order with your support team, clearly transmitted messages translate into profits.

Meet the Competition Head On

Ready to get your feet muddy? Are you prepared to do battle for the heart and business of a builder? Be forewarned: The battlefield doesn't have a second place. Come in second in this competition, and you lose.

Consider your competitor to be present in the marketplace to keep you from completing your sales plan. Your competition might raise questions about your ability to do a job or cast doubts about your products or services, your ability to make a shipment, or your service in the field. Competitors care little whether your company exists tomorrow or you have a job next week.

Competition is basic to life. Consider this story: Two hunters in the woods are surprised by a large grizzly bear. One turns to the other and sees him replacing his boots with running shoes. "You know a man can't outrun a grizzly," he says. Nodding in agreement, his friend says, "I don't care about outrunning the bear. I just want to outrun you."

Yes, competition is good for business, but it's a double-edged sword. Counteract the competition's strategy with one of your own, a strategy that represents your strengths and attacks their weaknesses. The sword's other edge proves more valuable: Competition keeps you and your firm at your best and winning the sale.

Step 1. Getting to Know Them

You can meet your competitors head to head and prevail in just two steps. Begin by getting to know your competition. Listen to a proven customer whom you're trying to convert to your product or service; he or she can detail your competition's true assets.

The builder will tell you the best thing about the current offerings and how they are serviced. Acknowledge the quality or level of strength of your competition. You can see the product in the field; pick up collateral material, owner's manuals, and the like; and begin to learn how that product works—a do-it-yourself course in features and benefits. Figure 5.1 provides a basic checklist for you to use in appraising the overall position of your competitors. In the war of the marketplace, information remains the ultimate ammunition. A rapidly growing array of products gets distributed to those selling to builders. Stay alert. Stay in touch with builders and with market trends. Keep listening and looking.

Use the form in Figure 5.1 to record information about your competitors. The information you gather will dictate strategies to counter their place in your market.

If your competition's trade contractors use generic products or commodity items such as lumber, insulation, roofing, and drywall, then installation and/or service matters. How do they install or construct? What are their specialties? What do you do differently? Take a photo of a job or several jobs that you competition has done. Set the photos alongside a representative sampling of your work or product. What makes your installation or your product look different, distinctive, better, more polished than the competitors'? The builder will be an excellent judge. The builder's reaction can help you understand what aspects of the product or installation are important to him or her.

How clean is your competitors' equipment? How polite or competent do they seem? How clean do they leave their jobsites? Recall the information provided in Chapter 4. How do they measure up against your image in the field? If time permits, take the builder by some of your jobs. Builders often ride through developments looking at the work being done by other builders.

Can you name your competition's weaknesses? What do they have difficulty doing? If the competition are suppliers, they could lack sufficient inventory or be unable to get to a job when the builder needs it. A service-related company may have a reputation for unreliability or have difficulty delivering goods or services on time, if at all. If a competitor does installation, then one of its weaknesses could be a lack of people power to get the job done in time to meet the builder's schedule. How does your company stack up against your competitors' weaknesses?

Step 2. Field Assessment

The second strategy comes when you meet your sales counterpart in the field or perhaps a driver or service technician. For instance, take time to observe—and learn from—how drivers or service technicians work. Do their vehicles stay clean and organized? Do they?

What kind of attitude or expertise is shown? If you are a trade contractor, you may well have begun your career working for another company alongside these people. They are great people to get to know, and these relationships allow you to put a face on your competitor. Each competitor has the same basic needs as you do. By seeing your competitor up close you realize that he or she is not superhuman after all. If you are active in your local home builders association, you can see how your competitor operates in a crowd and relates in committee meetings—generally observe how he or she handles things. That way, the competition becomes a person or two, rather than just a brand name.

FIGURE 5.1 Competitor Checklist

Company _____

Age of company _____ Estimated annual sales _____ Number of locations _____

# of trucks (locally) _____ Size of sales staff _____ Size of local location _____

Competing product lines:

_____   _____

_____   _____

_____   _____

_____   _____

_____   _____

Are key people certified? _____

Active in Home Builder's Association? _____

    Committees _____   Annual events _____ Newsletter _____

    Committees _____   Annual events _____

Active in which local markets: _____, _____, _____,

_____, _____, _____, _____

Reputation in the marketplace: _____

Installed sales offered? _____   Design services offered? _____

In-house service offered? _____

Biggest strengths: Biggest weaknesses:

_____   _____

_____   _____

_____   _____

_____   _____

_____   _____

Position in the marketplace _____

Last look bid position: _____

Do you know their costs? _____

Do they bundle? _____

Likewise, that person or persons gets to meet you. Okay? Now it's your turn to make a great impression because no doubt the boss will want to hear about you. Your attitude and intensity will set the stage for how you are viewed by your competitors.

How does your competitor handle the bidding process? Is he or she positioned to get first shot at a project or house, with you and any others brought in only to keep things honest? Or does your competitor wait until all bids have been received, then go to the builder and promise, "I'll beat your best bid by $XX.00's?" You will find this bit of information useful as you both approach new builders and try to keep your current builders as long-term customers.

Take this visualization a step further. If that person is in direct sales, imagine the individual at a desk or wherever he or she may be waiting to meet the boss or to discuss plans for how they are going to meet your advances in their territory. Visualize facial expressions or even words as he or she tries to explain the manner in which you are approaching the customer.

Imagine their disbelief as they receive the call or see the builder at the next job and learn that you have won the bid. Smile all the way to the bank.

When you get to know your competitors, you learn their strengths. They probably do many things well, but don't let that discourage you. What can you learn from them? Find out if they offer the standard for product/service in your area; how long they have been in business, and what they are doing right. If they are among the leaders, remember they did not get there overnight and without much time, effort, and money. All firms have strengths and weaknesses.

By listening to key customers and observing how they do business, you'll gain insight into finding your competitors'. What you do to exploit those strengths and weaknesses will help determine how well you will do in the market. Because you have assessed the needs of your prospect, your research should bear fruit here. Does your competitors' "armor" have a weak spot Was it that weak spot that gave you an opening to the builder in the first place?

If the builder seems especially concerned about a particular issue, ram that point home during your presentation. "Mr. Builder, let me make sure that I understand before I get back with you: Your current supplier of _____ has been taking two weeks to take care of quality check items. That delay is causing you more calls from homeowners who are becoming more irritated by the slow response time. Did I hear correctly?"

You counter the efforts of a competitor with your firm's unique strengths. Take the lead because, in many instances, you are your company in the field. Use your company's assets. If you are with an established company that knows the local market, you are already at a disadvantage. Your company has paid a price in marketing to and serving builders over the years. Call it tradition or market presence, the builder knows your reputation.

Assuming that the image is a strong one, use your reputation as one of your main points in discussions with the builder. Become familiar with strong builders who are already purchasing or using your services and drop some names. These testimonies are invaluable for referrals. Builders talk to builders about who gets the job done.

If you are opening a new location for a large company, be aware that strategies that may have worked elsewhere will not necessarily be useful here. Markets have different dynamics; be sure to fit your plan to this one. If you are fortunate enough to represent a brand name, then by all means take advantage of that good reputation.

If you are with a small company or work for a large enterprise with enlightened leadership, you could offer versatility. If you are quick enough to respond, the sale becomes yours. The benefits and features of your product line will help distance you from your competitor. Are all 2 × 4s the same? Carpet, appliance packages the same? Are all cabinet lines and bath fixtures the same? Does the market offer computer-aided design systems and computer accounting systems without individual distinction?

Of course not, you say. But if builders perceive suppliers as being basically the same, what can your firm do to distance itself from the competition? The same is true for the trades. In my 25 years of working with builders, I have never met a trim carpenter who did not say that his or her work was the best in the area. Quality first.

What counts is your proven ability to understand the unique needs of each builder and respond to those needs in a timely fashion. The last word is persevering. Stay around, even if that particular builder does not buy. Stay visible. One day your competitor will stumble just a little, and the builder may decide to try someone else for a while. If you have stayed close, you will have a golden opportunity not only to get that one sale, but those that follow.

Figure 5.2 provides a format to track your daily efforts to meet your competitors head on. Take advantage of this little form, and over a month's time you may be surprised at all you have done to grow your business. It is the little things that, when executed over time, add up to more builders doing business with you.

FIGURE 5.2 Today I Made Life Interesting for My Competitors By ...

Date	Feats of Daring Do

6

The Sale

Now the real fun begins. All your preparation and planning come into play and you do what you do best and enjoy most: sell to the builder. You'll find several references in this chapter to a survey I conducted to gain information about builders' buying habits. Part of the survey was carried out on the Internet; the rest of the information was gathered from participants in workshops I conducted with local builders associations in the Southeast and Midwest. I received a generous amount of assistance from home builders association executive officers who gathered information from their builder members.

Whether you contact a builder in person or by telephone, initially you'll need to follow a few basic guidelines. If you are a veteran in selling to builders, you know you need to think like builders do whenever possible. Look at the world through their eyes. They could care less about your difficulty in finding dependable labor, stalls in transportation, labor slow-downs at the manufacturer, or key employees calling in sick or just not showing up for work. They need the material they ordered to be at the jobsite now, and they want it installed when they need it. No excuses.

Members of your network and trade contractors you meet on other jobs will tell you what a particular builder considers important. Members of your network who have successfully sold their products or services to the builder in the past know what is important.

Before you make your sales call, remember to think like a builder. Try to have answers ready for questions the builder might ask. If you are just starting to sell to this market, try listing the questions you think you might be asked and have that information readily available. If you're a trade contractor, a builder might ask you to include in the contract the amount of insurance and worker's compensation coverage you carry. Be ready to answer the following questions immediately:

- Do you carry all the locally mandated licenses?
- How long have you been in business?

- Have you installed products on or built this particular style of house before?
- What kind of lead-time do you need to get crews to the jobsite?
- What are your response times to call backs?
- How many crews do you have?
- Do you work directly with your crews or do you have a lead person?
- Do they work for you or do you subcontract for their services?
- Are you a member of the local home builders association or other professional trade organizations?
- Do you get referrals from other builders in the area?

If you supply material, the list of questions might include:

- How long have you been in business?
- Do you deliver?
- Does your company have minimum order requirements for deliveries?
- What is your return policy?
- Do you have early morning deliveries?
- What are your lead times for deliveries and special-order products?
- Who services the product once installed?
- Do you provide specifications, testing data on the product, and installation diagrams?
- Do you offer installation of the product?
- Have you ever installed the product yourself?
- Is someone available locally to show my crews how to install the product?
- What are the rough-opening sizes?
- Do you sell to any builders in the area?

When you're selling to builders, the process begins with understanding the size of the operation. Size dictates how you reach the decision-maker. To get to the one who says yes, you sometimes must go through a gatekeeper, a person who sifts through the builder's calls and inquiries and who holds the key to your initial opportunity to meet with the builder. The gatekeeper might be a spouse, a receptionist, or a superintendent. Listen well and learn how this person sees his or her role in the organization. Maintain clear communication with all gatekeepers; know their names and something about them, and treat them with respect. Regardless of the volume of work a builder does, you'll need some basic items close at hand before you make your approach. Figure 6.1 Effective Sales Kit Checklist, provides you with some items to review.

Make sure the samples are in working order. Nothing leaves a poorer first impression than having a sample fall apart in your hands while you are extolling the product's virtues. Be prepared to leave a sample or video with prospective builders or purchasing managers.

Basic Selling Techniques

When you sell to a builder, you must tailor your approach to his or her sales volume. The chart in Figure 6.2 offers basic approaches to each of three sales volumes as well as to builders who impact your market but are not single-family.

FIGURE 6.1 Effective Sales Kit Checklist

	Pre-Call	1st Call	2nd Call	Close
Sales Kit				
Three Business Cards				
Credit Application				
Pricing				
Appliance Catalog				
Delivery Addendums				
Quick Quote Form				
Self-Addressed Envelope				
Presentation Form				
Competitive Information (Catalogs & Quotes)				
Client Management Folder				
Awareness of Customer Needs				
Promotion Material				
Prospective Customer Sheet				
Hats, Pens, Shirts				
Video				
Comparison Profiler				
Miscellaneous				

How to Approach the Small-Volume Builder

Many small-volume builders (1–25 houses a year) operate out of offices in their homes. It's a safe bet that they make some of their decisions at the kitchen table or standing outside a vehicle. Be ready to present your products or services in such an environment.

Keep it simple. If you have done your research well, you already have a good idea of the builder's needs and expectations. Your opening statement sets the stage: "Mr. or Ms. Builder, I am Stan Smith, and I work with builders who want to ..." If you were referred to the builder, make that clear early on. "Mr. Johnson, I was talking to

FIGURE 6.2 Sales Approaches by Volume

Method	Sales Volume		
	Small	Medium	Large
Cold Call	Yes	Sometimes	No
Sales Kit	Yes	Yes	Yes
Introduction Letter	Yes	Yes	Yes
Purchasing Manager	No	Possible	Yes
Multiple Layer	No	No	Possible

a friend of yours just last evening, and Bill Benton asked me to stop by. He said that you were needing or looking for _____."

Of the builders that responded to my survey, referrals were the fifth most positive way for new trades or suppliers to move into their realm of business. Much of the exploratory portion of any sales presentation becomes unnecessary with the builder because he or she draws certain assumptions based on the person who recommended that you make the call. If you are not following a referral, come prepared with a list of open-ended and closed questions that you need answered. A good list is contained in the opening section of this chapter.

A small-volume builder is an excellent candidate for onsite cold calling. Cold calls are the riskiest method of contacting a prospective builder, but they offer potentially the quickest return. That's especially true if you provide a product the builder needs at the time you are there. If you supply materials or services that are used in the construction process, refer to the construction time line in Figure 1.6 to gauge when the builder will require your product or service. Forecast the builder's need in sufficient time to deliver whatever you offer.

In a cold call situation, don't try to pin the builder down about a product or service that won't be required for months. The builder can make decisions on the spot; take note of the pending need and anticipate when you should get back in touch. Ask when a good time would be to follow through on the conversation. The builder will appreciate your attention to detail and may give you a date. The success of this effective technique comes from personal experience as well as observations of other successful sales professionals who have employed it.

If you do not have a referral for this prospect, look for clues to the builder's interest. Bumper stickers or items worn by a builder such as hats, shirts, or jackets may offer clues to favorite sports teams or other interests. If no evidence presents itself and you have no knowledge of the builder through your network, be prepared to discuss, even on a basic level, a concern of local, regional, or national interest. It could be the weather (too much rain, not enough, its impact on the building cycle), zoning issues, water and sewer services, building inspectors, and the like.

Just remember that you will in all likelihood be pulling the builder away from precious production time. Make your stop worth his or her time.

As you step out of your vehicle, you both make assumptions about each other. Are you just another salesperson or trade contractor looking for work? The builder will make several assumptions in the seconds before you utter your first word. Make sure those first impressions are good ones. The builder will assess the condition of your vehicle (cleanliness, paint job, dents, material, and tools), your manner of dress, your age, gender, and attitude. Your facial expressions say much about you. What image do you want to project?

The assumptions begin when the door to your vehicle swings open. If you keep your vehicle well organized and well maintained, the remainder of your latest meal will not come tumbling out, nor will papers go flying about the jobsite. A lack of clutter will generate a feeling of comfort for the builder. These opening minutes are about image and first impressions: You are your company on the jobsite.

After your initial greeting, keep your presentation tight and to the point. If some member of your network has told you about a situation that has arisen, be prepared to meet that need. She needs a dependable plumber now. His lumber package always shows up short from his present supplier. Her drywall contractor takes too long to take care of quality check items. My survey indicates that price was not always the issue with builders of this volume. Service is critical. Can you deliver and keep him or her within budget? Will your product or service be more reliable or cost-efficient? For builders, time equals money.

The interest clock ticks 24 hours a day, seven days a week. Your organization and product knowledge show during these high-pressure calls. Do you have handy the necessary material to answer questions? Can you lay your hands on it easily? If you cannot answer a question off the top of your head, impress the builder by reaching into your vehicle and finding it immediately. Good organization tells a builder he or she can trust you not to lose an order. It also sends a strong signal that you will follow through with the details.

Don't be afraid to leave a price list with this type of builder on the first call. If you carry a price list or catalogue with pricing, hand it over if the signs seem right. Your knowledge of the pricing structure in your market will pay off when the builder recognizes that your offering is competitive. This awareness cuts down on the games that are sometimes played between a builder and suppliers or tradespeople. If you need promotional pricing or have to meet an off-price situation, use the Quick Quote Form in Figure 6.3. This procedure works for medium-volume builders as well. Your quick and decisive action will demonstrate that you are a competent player and have the authority to commit on the spot.

Two words of caution at this point in the proceedings: One, if the builder quickly changes to your product or service, find out why. It may be your great timing, or the builder may be aggravated with the current supplier or trade contractor. Second, if the builder readily discloses the price offered by the current supplier or trade contractor, he or she will more than likely show your price to the next salesperson that comes along.

After completing the call, record your impressions on the Prospective Builder Form and include those valuable notes on what needs follow-up along with a date and time. Either later that evening or the next day mail a thank-you note to the builder for his or her time.

How to Approach the Medium-Volume Builder

A medium-volume builder (26 to 100 units per year) may have a small support staff. The gatekeeper can tell you the best time to call for an appointment. The builder's superintendent may be the first strong field contact you have. Superintendents often ferret out information for the builder and in some cases make decisions on products and services. My survey indicates that 10 percent of the time it's the superintendent who decides which goods and services to buy. Even if this field contact does not have direct decision-making authority, he or she will be a strong voice in the process. The jobsite superintendent has direct contact with what must happen each day for production to run smoothly. The wise builder listens to his or her superintendent. If this is the case, use the same presentation strategy as for a small-volume builder.

FIGURE 6.3 Quick Quote Form

Your Company Information Here

☐ **QUOTE**

☐ **SALES ORDER**

DATE _____

JOB NAME- ADDRESS _____

_____

SALESMAN _____

QTY.	UNIT	PART NUMBER	DESCRIPTION	UNIT PRICE	AMOUNT
				SUBTOTAL	
				TAX	
				TOTAL	

Above-Listed Prices Honored for _____

The ability to take advantage of national supplier volume rebates separates medium-volume builders from smaller ones. The field superintendent may not be aware of these potential rewards, but the builder will know about them. These rebates, in the form of promotional dollars or credits, aid a builder in marketing homes or outfitting a new model. If the builder does not relay that information to the superintendent, it may come from the person who tracks accounts payable. If your company represents a product or service that has such a program in place, make sure you have a list of the builders in your area who have signed up. If you have none, get a copy of the requirements for builders as well as for your company. Your network may let you know if such discounts are important to a particular builder.

If the medium-volume builder you are targeting employees a purchasing manager, you'll want to use an approach similar to that for a large-volume builder; see the next section for suggestions. Regardless, there are some aspects of how this volume builder does business that sets them apart from the other categories. Questions you need to answer to sell to this volume builder include:

- Are you capable of supplying a builder at this level? Are you willing to keep sufficient amounts of inventory on hand? Does your company have a sufficient number of crews or trucks to make deliveries or install the product in a timely fashion?
- Do you have the necessary capital or lines of credit available to support this volume builder until the job is finished and you are paid?
- Do you have the time to make necessary onsite contacts for service and punchout? Builders at this level often do not have the large-volume builder's human resources to perform quality check and after-sales warranty work.

Do you have the time or staff to take care of this for the builder? How an account is serviced is critical to medium-volume builders. My survey results showed that a supplier or trade contractor's in-house service department was the fifth most important criteria in making a buying decision. The survey also indicated that builders at this level look for salespeople to visit jobsites on a weekly basis, the decision-maker on a weekly basis (27 percent) or as needed (24 percent). The more a builder spreads out over a given geographic area, even at this volume level, the bigger your challenge in keeping up. Make sure you can deliver what you promise. Record this and other key information in the Prospective Customer Sheet (Figure 6.4).

As part of your gathering exercise, visit jobsites and be familiar with the builder's product line. While there speak with onsite salespeople or real estate agents who handle the marketing of the homes, trade contractors, and laborers on the jobsites. You need a strong, basic understanding of how they operate in the field. The sales approach remains the same as with a large-volume builder. The possible exception is that, in a medium-volume operation the builder may make the buying decisions; a large-volume builder usually relies on a purchasing manager.

How to Approach the Large-Volume Builder

Large-volume builders (101 units or more per year) are more formal in their decision-making processes. They will have a gatekeeper, perhaps more than one, so be prepared

FIGURE 6.4 Prospective Customer Sheet

PROSPECTIVE CUSTOMER SHEET

Name		Key Contact		

Address		City		Zip

Phone	Fax	Cell	Pager	E-Mail

Best Time to Call	Best Time to Call	Best Time to Call	Best Time to Call	Gatekeeper

Builder	Remodeler	Multi	Misc (Specify)

CURRENT SUPPLIER	Product	Product	Product	Product

Lead Source

DATE	PRODUCT	ACTIVITY	F/T

to make several attempts to get through. Once you have a name, try dropping off or mailing a letter introducing yourself and explaining what you do. The more polished the letter, the better your chance of getting an interview. If you're writing because you have a referral from a builder or a current supplier or trade contractor, be sure and mention that person's name in the first paragraph.

The purchasing manager may have multiple roles and therefore little time for empty chatter. For large-volume builders, the purchasing manager makes buying decisions for the entire house, tracks and changes specifications, and looks for new and improved building methods. He or she stays perpetually short of time. Be a great resource and make their lives simpler with (a) your knowledge of your products, (b) an appreciation for where you fit into the building process, and (c) contacts with other suppliers and tradespeople who can meet the needs of builders at this volume.

Follow the letter with a call. Ask the receptionist for the best time to set up an appointment; the manager may designate certain days for considering new products and services. This volume builder may have a group of marketing, sales, and production people who review new products. Determine the process and adapt accordingly. If someone is involved in addition to the purchasing manager, include sufficient material for the internal presentation.

Set your appointment directly with the gatekeeper, and record the date and time on your calendar. If you have the time, send him or her a letter or e-mail of thanks for taking time to see you and say you are looking forward to the meeting. Pictures of your product or service help in the absence of samples.

Produce your own pictures of local applications. Be prepared to have available marketing support funds (for preset ads, television or radio advertising scripts or newspaper inserts). Model home programs provide the accepted norm in many markets. If you do not have such a program, prepare one in advance of your meetings. Members of your network who are currently doing business with the builder and have model home programs as part of their offerings will let you know if the builder will expect you to do the same. Model home programs for material and services often include:

- a reduced price for what you supply or install in the home
- extended credit terms for a builder
- deeper discounts if the builder includes upgraded materials above what the builder normally orders
- incentives that reward the builder for sales from the model (An incentive could be free or reduced prices on products on the 10th, 20th, or 40th, etc. house built in a given year.)
- advertising allowances that support mixed-media marketing, which is often based on projected sales

This list counts among the ways some suppliers can support the use of models by a builder. The construction and maintenance of a model remains the single-most expensive line item in a builder's advertising budget. Don't be discouraged by the length of time it takes a large-volume builder to make a decision. Decisions often involve multiple people and multiple levels of responsibility. Some large-volume builders restrict the presentation of products and services to specific times of year.

If you are not there or are not on the notification list, you'll miss your opportunity for another year. If that happens, make sure your name appears on the list for the next bidding period, and note this important date on your calendar. If you consider it critical to have business from this builder in the future, use the extra time to gather intelligence by visiting present and future jobsites. Talk to the builder's current tradespeople.

Presentation Preparation for Medium- and Large-Volume Builders

Take sufficient time prior to the appointment to make sure that you and your materials are ready. Do you have everything on your Effective Sales Kit Checklist? Before you make the presentation, decide what are you willing to do to obtain the sale. Take a sheet of paper and draw a T. Place on the left those items you need to get the sale: credit application, list of projects, proper lead times, delivery and service expectations, list of key personnel with telephone and fax numbers and e-mail addresses, liability questions answered, signed contract. On the right, place items you are willing to give up get the sale. These items would include price concessions, model home discounts, volume discounts, promotional assistance, price protection, and such. This information becomes important when the presentation turns into a negotiation. Know your choices up front.

Take time to check your appearance. Follow the locally acceptable dress code (some territories or company policies dictate coat and tie or a woman's business suit over dress casual . Avoid any loose strings, wrinkled shirts or blouses, dirty shoes, etc. Don't let anything detract from what you're saying. If in doubt about proper attire, ask yourself how your biggest competitor would dress.

Once the appointment has been made, be on time. Too early (15 minutes or more) gives the sense that you're rushing the purchasing manager. Instead, sit in the parking lot and review your material until closer to the appointment time. If you are running late, call and make sure that you can arrive later than scheduled.

When you arrive in the reception area, look for clues to the builder's nature. An increasing number of builders display their mission statements, framed pictures of developments or products, and framed or laminated articles about their businesses from newspapers and magazines. These displayed items provide clues to the character of the company. If the builder took the time and expense to have these items framed, they carry meaning. Note them.

Turn your pager to vibrate, and leave your cell phone in the car or turn it off. If you need a telephone to do some immediate questions or follow-up, ask to use the builder's. Nothing appears ruder than taking a call while making a presentation or while treating a builder to a meal.

The key person in the presentation phase for these two volume levels remains the purchasing manager. This important contact comes to the job from two basic approaches. He or she may have served in the field as a builder/superintendent. The field makes a great training ground for the job and provides valuable experience for the years ahead. Not only did the builder/superintendent have to meet production schedules, but he or she had to deal with all the frustrations that come with products or services that are well sold but poorly delivered and installed. Be prepared for a different line of questions if the purchasing manager has a field background.

A second career path is that of the professionally trained manager. This person may come to the job from a similar position in another industry. Others train by taking business school courses. Either way, expect questions that are drawn from limited experience with the practical application of products from those who have had to deal with products and applications in the field. These questions may be more of a technical nature.

The Presentation

You are now at center stage. After the usual greetings, pleasantries, and the ritual of the business card exchange, you are ready to begin. Thank the purchasing manager for taking time out of a hectic schedule to meet with you. Your next words can be a 30-second description of what you do or supply and why the builder should consider using you. "These samples or brochures or charts indicate what we do. What can we do to make you more profitable, efficient, stronger, larger?" Then listen. What does the manager say he or she needs? Ask opened-ended questions that require more than a yes or no answer.

"How are your sales looking for this year?"

"How is the sewer moratorium affecting future development?"

"What are your needs on the Four Winds project?"

"How will the addition of tap-on fees impact our industry?"

"Describe for me the ideal supplier or trade contractor for your company."

The answers to these questions and others will come out of the give-and-take in business conversation. The information they provide will give you greater insight into the builder's requirements while verifying information you have received from research, your network, and visits to the jobsite. Attitudes will surface. Listen for buzz words or catch phrases; they'll tell you what the builder considers important. Quality is likely to come up and perhaps craftsmanship or tradition. How does the building firm see itself in the community and among other builders? What expectations does the management express about suppliers or trade contractors? What delivery schedules? Is management looking for extended credit terms or rebates and perhaps advertising allowances? Are national buying agreements currently in place?

Clarify the purchasing process during these opening exchanges. Is it solely that person's decision or are others involved in a committee or group? Ask what kind of timeline is part of the decision-making process.

As you gather information, glance around the room and take note of wall decorations. Plaques, diplomas, pictures of family and hobbies, or cartoons are generous clues as to what this person finds really important. How organized does he or she appear? Will your bid get lost in the piles? If he or she seems scattered, make your material colorful and bulky so it will be easy to find. You are gathering good information for conversation and more information about who the purchasing manager is and perhaps what motivates him or her.

When making the presentation, listen for key words that will give you clues as to how they will receive information. Visual people use phrases such as "Let's look at what you have," "Our company looks at the big picture in market," and "What you have looks interesting."

Auditory persons use words such as, "I hear that you are . . ." "A builder told me that you frame . . ." "It sounds like you have . . ."

Tactual people use words like, "I feel certain that we . . ." ". . . we are trying to get our hands on." "I'll touch base with you . . ." "A builder in Smithville thinks that you . . ."

Observe the person's body language. Does he or she—

- Look at you while talking?
- Look at you when you are making a point?
- Sit back in the chair with arms folded or come forward and lean on the desk or table?
- Take notes?
- Respond to your questions? How? With a nod, smile, or lifted eyebrow? Your answers to these questions are all signals as to how effectively you communicated to that person's particular style of receiving information. Read *How to Read a Person Like a Book*, a good basic study of body language, by Nierenberg and Calero[4]. These two experts say that up to 80 percent of our person-to-person communications are nonverbal.

Become familiar with what a person says with body language, and be aware of yours:

- How well are you listening?
- How are you responding to information? With a nod, a smile?
- Are you taking notes? Notes are our way of showing that what is being said is important enough to record.
- Do you look him or her in the eye when you are talking?
- Are you sitting back? Let your body language match that of your contact. If he or she leans back, lean back yourself. If the purchasing manager leans on the table, you lean too. If he or she yawns, you may have overstayed your welcome.

The answers to your questions and your observations of the overall environment enable you to know a great deal about the individual with whom you are speaking. Your responses show you know what you're talking about. You gain credibility. Good job!

Remember this simple phrase when presenting your product or service: So what? Successful sales trainer Tom Bychinski of Wausau, Wisconsin, emphasizes this point: You need to think ahead like a builder does. Unless the builder can see a way your product or service will meet the needs he or she shared with you, then you're the only one who's going to be excited. If the feature doesn't meet the needs of the builder or the home buyer, you're wasting your breath.

- You offer your multiple windows factory mulled. . . . So what?
- You have service people available within 48 hours of a call. . . . So what?
- You offer no-wax floors in 18 colors, all in stock. . . . So what?
- Your crews clean-up after their jobs everyday. . . . So what?
- You offer next-day delivery. . . . So what?

Again, through your research identify a real benefit that fits the builder's or home buyer's need. Explain the benefit behind the feature to the builder. If the builder responds with, "So what?" you need to answer, "Because of this feature, Mr. or Ms. Builder, your home buyer will know that you have chosen the most powerful in its class." "Because of this feature, Mr. Builder, your home owners will increase the value of their home." "Because of this feature, Ms. Builder, your home owner will experience a feeling of security that is not available with the other products on the market."

Listening to the purchasing manager's "so what" questions and observing his or her body language allows you to explain how this information or these features will help them sell more houses. Long-time sales-to-builder professional John Hamrick says once you know how the builder sells, you sell him or her the same way.

Making a direct comparison to what is currently used has proven an excellent means to make your point. Create a simple but effective chart that reflects what is important to the builder or home buyer. If you have electronic display devices available, you can use some of the increasing amount of material produced by national suppliers and available through local contacts. Chose to show pictures of how you install product compared to your competition. Don't downgrade your competition; the charts and pictures will be clear enough. Establish what the differences are, so your price will be justified. "Mr. or Ms. Builder, is this a great value or what?"

When you show what you have done and can do for them, the creative side of the builder emerges. What new possibilities exist for the builder's homes using your product or service? How much more versatile will your service or product allow the builder to be? We have become a choice-driven culture; the more choices, the greater the chance of success for both you and the builder. Getting him or her to invest in the creative process using what you propose to provide with expanded choices puts you a giant step closer to closing the sale. You and the builder are becoming a team. Builders invest their most precious commodity—their time—with you and, during the creative process, their energy.

Occasionally you'll get a question that you cannot answer with the material at hand. Try looking the builder in the eye and saying, "Great question. In my experience, I have never run across that question before. Could I have a hour, day, or week to get that answered for both of us and get back to you?" "Could I call you this coming Tuesday with the information?" Requesting a specific amount of time allows you to gain agreement from the builder while maintaining a sense of urgency. Make sure you allow yourself enough time. Answering the question gives you a great opportunity to follow-up with something of substance. Few sales have been lost to truthfulness; you have too much at stake to make up material or fake an answer.

Negotiation

As you begin the question-and-answer portion of your presentation, you can either get the sale or set up the close by using basic negotiation tactics. You have already determined during your preparation time what you think or have learned through research, and what you are willing to concede to close the sale. The self-imposed pressure of having to get the sale at any cost will come through in how you handle yourself under pressure. If you press too hard the manager will not respond in a positive manner. If he or she gets the idea that you must have this sale, forget about negotiating. You may get the sale, but on the building company's terms. Don't be intimidated by the décor or atmosphere in the office where you are meeting.

Approach prospective builders or purchasing managers with the attitude that while the sale is important, it is not a matter of life or death. Your confidence in yourself, your product or service, and your company's ability to deliver as needed will come through. Don't give away anything you haven't decided on beforehand.

Take advantage of this time of give-and-take to discuss the value-added benefits of doing business with your firm. What do you have beside price that offers value to the builder? Your homework has supplied most of this information. If the manager asks for something at this stage that you did not anticipate but can do within reason, then agree. The value-added possibilities your company could have include—

- more trucks and crews than others in your trade.
- the most experienced craftspeople in the area.
- first-of-day delivery by 7:30 a.m.
- local showroom in which to display options to homeowners.

Present the price last by taking the prospect through the process. If asked for price early on, you can still make the point of what you are offering at that price by saying, "Have I understood you to say you want to have the jobsite cleaned every day, and for us to have worker's compensation insurance? Our crews are not to park in driveways and not to use water from neighboring homes. Did I hear correctly?" "Do I understand that you will need your callbacks taken care of in 48 hours? We will commit to you that we will keep key products in stock for immediate backup."

"You will be pleased with our prices. Did I understand you to say that the following were important (enumerate those items while looking for nods or words of acknowledgment.) "Your firm can have all of that for $_____. How does that fit within your budget?"

If you have done your homework you'll know the basic price levels and terms that are common in your market. You'll have a solid knowledge of expectations from listening to trade contractors and members of your network. You have visited jobsites and know the builder's homes. List the offerings that separate you from your competition. Make your value-added advantages part of the total package and pricing.

Expect some objections to come via the purchasing manager. The purchasing manager's responsible for getting the best product and service for the dollar while staying within a specified budget. Approach objections by:

- Restating the objection as you heard it, making sure you understand what is being expressed. Make sure of your facts. If the objective is outlandish, just hearing the objection repeated back can often turn it in your favor.
- If you have a readily available answer, respond by saying, "Good point. I only get that question from those who are really sharp or conscientious enough to . . .
- Respond with the benefits and features of what you are offering. Explain what makes you different from your competition. Why choose you?
- Restate those benefits in terms that tie in with needs the builder has expressed. When you use terms that fit the prospect's particular communication style, it show that you're listening to what the builder is saying and applying those needs

to a solution. Use charts to compare products and services. If you cannot get charts from your sources, make up your own. Take your biggest competitors and look up the 10 most critical features needed by the builder. Use printed material from your competition that lists the ratings, etc. "While this chart does not list all that you have said is important, it does show some key points. Are they not critical to you?"

■ Answer a question with a question. "How often do you need crews on the job at 7 a.m.?" "What size is the hardest for most of the suppliers you have dealt with to stock, and how often do you need it?" " No, sir, we do not charge freight on special orders when we have sufficient time to have them top loaded with our regular orders."

■ Be aware of the possibility of what I call the X-factor in negotiating. The builder may have a long-standing personal relationship with the current supplier or trade contractor that transcends business. Those bonds are difficult to fracture, particularly if your competitor is doing the job needed for the builder.

The Close

With perfect timing and a builder who needs what you are offering, you may get the sale that day. Again, questions will help a builder make that decision. "We are placing our next order on Monday. With your permission I could include your first order and have it here in time for your open house." Or, "We are currently scheduling field audit teams and can have one in place in two weeks. Does that fit your time frame?" "You said a few minutes ago that you needed to have the house trimmed out in time to meet a June 15 closing. We can get that done if we begin next Tuesday." "You seem to indicate that you are dissatisfied with your present trade or supplier but are not sure if we can meet your standard. Please allow us to ship to the next house in Highland Glen and see how we do what we say. You be the judge." Don't be afraid to ask for the sale. Price may well be an objection. My survey indicates that builders consider competitive price the second most important criteria in the purchasing process. The need to have the lowest price was sixth. One builder of multifamily projects recently told me that, for him, competitive means two bids of equal value in product offering and about 5 percent different in price.

Let me share a word of experience here. Your competition may have already been in to see the purchasing manager and may not have given the bid the attention to detail that you have. Perhaps he or she missed an elevation or misread a spec. If you do your research, follow the same requirements as your competition, and still find a great difference in price, question the validity of the figures presented to the builder.

"Excuse me, sir, did they include _____ and did they meet your need for _____?" Your suspicions may prove to be correct. By asking direct questions you show familiarity with your product and its positioning in your area. You may save the purchasing manager a lot of time. If you are bidding against the current supplier or trade contractor, you may find yourself at a disadvantage on certain products. Estimates for framing packages, trim packages, siding or brick takeoff, drywall, and floor covering, for instance, are not always as accurate using a blueprint takeoff as an estimate done by a crew that has built or installed the product on the same elevation several times. You may ask for the exact amount of material supplied (no dollars are mentioned or needed if you have done your homework) so as to provide the most accurate bid for comparison.

If you have presented your product or service by highlighting how certain features will benefit builders and/or homeowners, you have laid the groundwork for meeting the price objection. If you can also meet the product's service requirements, your price should stand on its own merit. If you have done your research to determine where your competition's price falls, then your quote will be accurate and will save much time in the bidding process.

Successfully completing these three steps will eliminate much of the back and forth between what the builder expects and what you have quoted. The quote gives you a measure of credibility with the builder and shows that you know what you are doing and what the product or service is worth in the builder's market.

Do not despair if price seems the only issue. Your ability to deliver the product or service in a timely fashion and your attention to details will soon follow. Savvy to the real world of field operations, those people in sales and service providers to the building community will mention the ability to follow through when problems arise.

As John Ruskin observed years ago, "There is hardly anything in the world that some men can't make a little worse and sell a little cheaper, and the people who consider price only are this man's lawful prey."[5] This comparison shows the relationship between the price and the product or service you offer.

Price, Product, or Service

Price is what a service or product is worth to the builder or his or her home owner. Value is how you deliver that worth to the builder, enhancing your product or service. It also justifies the price. It should reflect the specific needs of the builder.

> NEEDS = DELIVERED VALUE

The purchasing manager may not be able to make a decision that day and may require another meeting. You may use the initial sales call on this volume of builder to gather information for the quote. If so, schedule another appointment after considering the time required to answer their questions or do research. During that time, the builder may require you to fill out a Vendor Information Sheet and undergo a credit check. You may need to do a take-off from a plan. Schedule the next appointment now; if your instincts say the builder or purchasing manager seems interested, commit to a new time and come prepared with all their questions answered.

Once you are in your vehicle or back at your office, debrief yourself. Take notes on how you think the call went. Did it meet your expectations? Were there any surprises? Did you gather sufficient information to make a realistic quote? What do you need to do with your list of priorities to get ready for the next meeting? Did you discover issues that must be brought to those to whom you report? Be sure to follow through with any requests from the purchasing manager in a timely fashion. Your follow-through will say much about how you take care of information requests.

Many salespeople hate to do this chore, but it must be done to keep the engine of commerce running smoothly.

The Second Sales Call

You have already thanked the builder for the original sales presentation and noted the specific items that needed to be addressed. You established the time for your follow-up call while you were ending the first one. The arrival and preparation for this next call remains the same as for the first. What you bring may be different.

Take time to address the purchasing manager's questions. You have the opportunity of quoting the job. Do it right. The purchasing manager will have a budget figure in mind, or if you are replacing a current supplier, product line, or trade contractor, the manager will expect you to be in line with those numbers.

If the purchasing manager wants to get you and your company in the door he or she may reveal what budgets are in use. Be wary of new projects whose budget was established by an architect. Experience in the varied lines that I have represented over the years show that architect-based budgets are nearly always short of what is realistically needed.

If the bid includes an established specification for what you are quoting, you need few cautions. Just be accurate. Double-check or have someone else double-check your figures. Increasingly, software programs will do the task for you. But the old carpenter's rule still rings true: "Measure twice, cut once."

Be aware that your competition may choose to bid the job differently—or with the same sense of caution that you have. In several product and service categories, I have seen companies choose to ignore the builder's specifications and quote something less. Sometimes they are successful.

While you might have taken a general approach to product and services in the first call, you can now be specific. You may also have some knowledge of the purchasing manager's interest. If time permits, arrive with relevant articles of interest to the manager. (If the matter is time-sensitive, mail the items with a note attached.) Bring a memento as part of the return visit. Consider an item similar to one I have developed over the years—the purchasing manager's Survival Kit. It makes a great impression. After the normal business courtesies, begin by saying, "Jack or Jill, it is good to see you again. I have taken the time to research your questions and have some answers that will please you," or "We have met the specifications that you were looking for," or "addressed the concerns that we discussed last week."

Begin your presentation. Give sufficient time to make your points and allow reaction from the purchasing manager. How are you doing? Ask questions that clarify what you have presented and encourage your prospect to tell you that he or she understands it. If you have done similar work with builders the purchasing manager would recognize, mention them at this time.

If you have met the criteria, have enough information, and are comfortable with the proceedings, ask for the sale. When you get the order, be sure to hand carry the initial order through your system (in the case of a multiple-step company). Everyone along the line needs to know what to do and when. The credit department needs to have the builder's information before you ship the product. Order entry must have the exact details of what has been sold and when it is needed. Provide accurate and complete information to prevent the rush that often accompanies hasty sales; rush orders will stretch organizations of all sizes. Make sure the warehouse and/or delivery personnel have directions to the jobsite and emergency phone numbers in case they have questions.

Meet the truck for the first delivery. Get a reaction from the people installing your product for the first time. If your product installation has idiosyncrasies, have a pre-installation meeting with the people who will do the labor. Drop a line to the purchasing manager thanking him or her for the order. Repeat for the second sale as well.

Why repeat for the second sale? The first two deliveries show the real capabilities of your company and its ability to communicate. Despite your best efforts, something may happen that will shed a less than favorable light on you and your company. When you walk through the second order, you increase your chances of catching small glitches. This attention to detail lets those in your organization know the importance of this account. The builder will notice as well.

What happens if you do not get the sale? Stay in touch. Keep the decision-makers aware of what is going on with your company and the progress you are making. Ask them why you did not get the sale. This information will assist you and your company in obtaining future sales from this company and others. Stay friendly at home builders association functions, continue to visit jobsites, and stay in touch with trade contractors. The people who have the business may stumble. Change comes.

If you have stayed in touch, and the builder knows your capabilities, he or she will remember your face and name and will likely give you the first shot if the time comes for a replacement. When your competitor's service falls, you'll have a golden opportunity to rise—but only if you have stayed in touch. If the builder's business is important to you long-term, stay in touch.

Builders at all volume levels depend on their trade contractors to do the actual construction of the home. Few builders have their own on-payroll employees doing the actual building. If you are in a trade or supply material for building, these people are often overlooked as a valuable source of information. Consider them a part of your network; they are a strong contact to have.

Future Buying Trends

In one area close to my territory and in Northern Virginia, builders are grouping together and forming their own buying groups. For a trade contractor or supplier, having a group means having one contact instead of several. You may have less people to interact with as well from a customer service standpoint. These buying groups in many ways act like large-volume builders. The trend toward buying groups may be one means small-volume builders will employ in competing with their larger counterparts.

I hope that this chapter moved as quickly for you as one of your days selling to builders. Take time at the end of your busy day to savor the good that occurred and reflect on what you have learned. On days when you are making formal presentations you will need to allow a little more time than usual time between calls to review what you covered and to note the questions that still need to be answered. Every day that you can present your product or service is a good day. I trust that today was such a day.

Build Territorial Management Skills

Despite whether they like paperwork, most good salespeople have a system in place to keep track of important exchanges between themselves and builders. It may be as simple as a daily record of what has occurred, jotted down in a spiral note-book. It may be as sophisticated as a database kept on a personal computer, laptop, or hand-held computer. Regardless, consistently effective sales professionals use and maintain a system.

This chapter introduces the Client Management Folder, which allows you to keep relevant data in a single location. The Client Management Folder gives you the maximum amount of information in the minimum amount of space—and it allows easy access to that information.

Relationships?

Relationships cannot substitute for good products or services delivered on time at a competitive price, but they do matter. When pressed for a decision, builders often go not with the newest, lowest prices but with salespersons/trade contractors and companies that have met their needs in the past and are close in price.

While researching this book, I asked a number of associates what they wanted to see on this trade subject. The most-requested topic: building relationships with builders. So how do you do that? How do you build those lasting relationships? You build relationships just like you build a house. Begin by being patient; strong, long-term relationships take time to form. On rare occasions you may become fast friends with the builder right away.

Form your foundation on common interests. If you are from the same region of the country, you may already have items in common; you just need to discover what those interests are. Observe bumper stickers, caps, posters, and plaques on the builder's walls. You both may follow the same college or professional team. You may be part of the same community of faith. Your children may go to the same school or compete in the same conference. Or, your children may both participate in clubs, Scouts, or another youth-related activity. You both may enjoy the same recreational pursuits.

In the past, people were born, raised, married, and worked in a given region all their lives. No more. Families migrate from one area of the country to another, sometimes several times.

For instance, in the Southeast, the land of southern drawls, you can now hear the distinctive northeastern accent of builders, suppliers, and trade contractors. The trends toward migration and toward finding and bonding with folks from your "home" area offer a great opportunity to increase your business and friendship circles. I can't predict how many rounds of golf it will take or how many hot dogs you'll have to eat at a local college ballgame. I only know those rounds of golf and those hot dogs will be worth the effort for both of you.

This shared common ground will result in a state of mutual respect, which will then allow the next step to occur. Trust forms from respect, and it takes time. Trust evolves from performance over time and circumstance; both parties do what they say. You supply on time or apply on time, and with a minimum of trouble, and the builder pays you in a timely fashion.

If the trust has not developed yet, continue to be patient with the builder. More often, you and your company need time to prove you'll do what you say you will. My personal rule of thumb is the third sale.

By the third sale or job completed, the builder will be able to determine whether much of what you have been saying is true. Somewhere in the completion of the three sales or jobs, you will probably have a crisis or two to handle in a professional manner and to the liking of the builder.

The result will extend the relationship. You are not just a great person who holds some of the same interests as the builder; you are able to come through when the builder needs you most.

Common interests get you in the door, positive performance keeps you there. With that in mind, be prepared to do what is necessary to meet the builder's demands. You may need to make extra trips to the jobsite for late afternoon or Saturday deliveries, put in extra calls to your vendor, and provide consistent attention to a small detail. Do it. When asked, assertive builders will be more than willing to lay out their expectations for you.

With common interest, mutual respect, and trust comes an appreciation for the role that each of you plays in the building process. You respect the builder for his or her role in developing affordable housing in the community, while the builder respects you for the manner and means you employ to supply or apply products in his or her house. Both parties need each other to be successful. The resulting appreciation will allow you both to form common goals. How many houses will the builder construct over the next year? What can you do to help make that goal come alive and keep the builder profitable? One of the early signs of trust comes when the builder gives you a set of construction keys. These keys allow you and members of your company access to the house once it has been dried in and needs to be locked.

You might also find that with time and trust you take on the role of advisor in the building of a house. Along the way you will learn more about the builder's business plans and dilemmas. The builder will look to you for advice in handling situations or a challenge that falls outside his or her expertise.

You are the expert in your field, a valuable resource during and after construction. You have at your disposal various pieces of information about your products and services that the builder does not have. What available item might help builders construct houses in a more efficient manner? What ideas has your local vendor representative passed on to you that might help the builder? What ideas are being used with your product and service in other zones of the country that would be of benefit to builders in your market?

For builders, a long-term relationship brings reliability. Builders need for you to do what you say. Period. For the nearly 27 years I have been involved in the industry, a central concern that surfaces frequently during candid discussions with builders is the lack of reliability from trade contractors and suppliers.

Some companies or individuals don't seem to get the point. They are not aware of the need for continuity between what they say and what they do. As I pointed out in Chapter 1, builders resist change. That resistance applies not just to products, but to trade contractors as well.

Not many builders in the marketplace will change just for the sake of changing. Do you recall the chart in Figure 1.4 that showed the steps in the building process? When the steps go smoothly for the builder, the house produces more profit because time equals dollars. Changes cost money and eat up construction schedules. Knowing you can be relied upon to deliver what you promise—and on schedule—will keep the business.

Some builders in your market might always be on the lookout for a better deal; they would not be interested in building a relationship. Their criteria for success does not center on consistent suppliers and trade contractors. When you get their business, enjoy it while it lasts. If a builder changes quickly to go with you, someone else offering a better price will soon be on the doorstep asking for the builder's business. Members of your network can be most helpful in identifying these builders.

Less change makes the building process go more smoothly for the builder. And it makes your job easier. People within your organization who have direct contact with builders may love the routine of meeting established builder's expectations. Your sales support people will recognize a particular builder's voice. They know the idiosyncrasies that make that builder unique and often fun to work with. They will take pride in continually meeting this loyal customer's expectations.

The Client Management Folder

Section 1. Communication

Section 1 of the Client Management Folder relates to communication (Figure 7.1). Record the basic information every salesperson needs to maintain an account. This section may not change during the entire sales year. It contains crucial information about where and how to contact the builder, including the best time to do so.

Each builder has his or her own expectations about privacy; remember and respect them. Having children at home makes a difference: If school is in session,

FIGURE 7.1   The Client Management Folder

Client Management Folder

Builder

Address   State   Zip

Phone   Fax

Sales

Frequency

Class | 1996 | 1997 | 1998

Customer Since   In Business Since   Tax Exempt

Key Contacts

Bank Name   Loan Officer   Phone

Principal Information

Principal(s) Name   Birthday   Educ

Mobile   Pager

E-mail   Home

Spouse   Anniversary

Children

Awards, etc.

Recreation

Community Involvement

Politics   Religion

Drink   Music/Artist   Smoke

Favorite places for lunch

Dinner

Special needs/concerns

Passion/Hot Button

Conversation Starters

Best time to call

Gatekeeper Information

Services/Products File

	2000	2001		2000	2001
Jan			Jul		
Feb			Aug		
Mar			Sep		
1st Q			3rd Q		
Apr			Oct		
May			Nov		
Jun			Dec		
2nd Q			4th Q		
YTD			Total		

the parents will be up early. Ask the builder for the best time to call and the best number to use.

Section 2. Personal Information

This part of the Client Management Folder results from the need to record the increasing amount of personal data collected from the builder. Long-term relationships grow stronger when you pay attention to the important aspects of the builder's life. Modify this section to meet the specific lifestyles of the builders in your market. Much of this valuable information will come from conversations over the years and your mutual comfort in discussing the details of your lives.

I have a space for family information, including spouse and children, and important dates such as anniversary and birthdays. How important is education in the builder's background? If you see a school diploma or certificate of completion (such as the Graduate Builder Institute), take note. What school or college did the builder attend and may now support?

What awards have been won or offices held in the community? These achievements indicate what has gone into the builder's development as a person. What does he or she do for fun? What causes does he or she support in the community? Again, these awards provide strong clues to the individual's character and suggest causes you or your company might also want to or already support.

What is the builder's level of political involvement? Is it bumper sticker status, or is he or she active in the local home builders association's Political Action Committee or perhaps a local political party? What role does religion play? What are some of the builder's personal tastes? How about favorite places to dine? Should any special needs or concerns be addressed on a regular basis? What has the builder shared with you that may need particular emphasis by you or your company on a regular basis?

Section 3. Business Information

If you were to examine this information, how well would you know this account? In the 'frequency' space, note how often you need to see this builder: For simplicity's sake, the form classifies builders as weekly (1), bimonthly (2), monthly (4), or every six weeks. The next six zones allow you to record sales for the past three years. Note how long the builder has been a customer, and how long he or she has been in business. Key banking information can be obtained, if needed, because some types of builder-related sales, service, or installation need this data. His or her involvement in builder-related organizations comes next. As with the entire Client Management Folder, modify to your personal taste.

Section 4. Product-Driven

This section gives you a chance to record in one place what the builders buy and from whom in whatever categories you choose. Modify the zone to fit your company's specific requirements. If you or your company offer a variety of products and services, this section will give you ample exposure to what the builder is buying. It also allows you to stay focused on what you need to keep in front of the builder.

Section 5. Sales History

You can track sales here by month for two years. See at a glance where the account is going as you update it monthly. It will reveal how builders respond to your company's activities. The previous three-year history will help you determine which strategies need to be in place for you to increase sales.

Section 6. Notes

This three-page section provides a place for you to record frequent calls on or to the builder and what you need to do to for follow-up. Take time after each call to record what was worth remembering. The poorest note is better than the best memory. They are all in one place and easy to track.

Planning for a Successful Week

Effective sales professionals and trade contractors begin their week by planning. They avoid the time trap that trips those who sell to builders but don't have the first clue what they will sell during the coming week. Those people just head out Monday morning to call on builders who have been buying in hopes of catching a prospect along the way.

Effective sales professionals and trade contractors have learned that a scattered approach to selling often results in a midweek panic that comes from having too many immediate needs to respond to and no time to build the business for tomorrow. Planning in advance—using your Client Management Folder—will diminish the panic that comes when you lose control of your day.

Remember: You are in charge of your day. Begin the week with a fresh focus. Gather the notes collected from last week of what has to be done. When are you most productive? When are you best at selling? When are you best at solving problems?

Take advantage of your peak energy times to address such issues. The occasional interruption can be tolerated, but don't get caught in the time trap and be out doing something that takes your focus away from selling and seeing builders. A 2- to 4-hour planning session at the beginning of the week allows you to—

- Do the most unpleasant tasks first. Then that dread won't gather momentum and get in the way of more productive time during the balance of the day. If you are required to do something in response to a previous contact with a builder, you have nearly all day to finish, instead of putting off the call and having the deadline be impossible to meet.
- Make sure that all issues from last week have been handled. If not, this planning session offers a great opportunity to address them with all parties, as well as to follow up on items already in place that the builder will ask about during the course of the week. . . . for example, that pesky part or back order that will not go away as you intended?

- You are in one place for an extended period of time. That eliminates the "telephone-tag" that often occurs when trade contractors or salespeople are on the move and unable to be at one phone number for any length of time. You can take advantage of your cellular line and land line during the same period of time. By devoting one to outgoing calls and one to incoming, you will not have to wait for call backs to keep your day on track.

In reality, those of us who use integral radio and cellular units as well as conventional cell phones can keep as many as three related conversations going at once. While it may sound a little unreal, circumstances often dictate the use of all three—in the office, of course, not on the road. A growing number of builders and remodelers use e-mail as part of their correspondence. If that's the case with your customer base, take advantage of this time and update your files.

- Do you have any meetings of the local home builders association or any other professional association this week? Allow 120 minutes for every 60-minute meeting. An extra 30 minutes provides for the inevitable chitchat before and after a committee meets; use this time for networking. Allow at least 30 minutes for driving to and from the location.
- Do you have any sales presentations this week? What materials do you need? Are your samples in order? Have you called or written to the builder verifying the date and time?
- What key prospects do you need to see this week? Do they require an appointment? If your goal, for instance, is to increase your business base by 20 percent, then you need to add an extra 5 percent for those along the way who say "no."
- Do you need to think through how you present a familiar product? Even old products take on freshness when presented in a new way. Manufacturers continue to crank out new and improved products during the year. Review what you discovered in your reading last week that would benefit your builders this week and prepare to pass on the information.
- Write and mail that letter thanking a prospective builder for the appointment last week, or say thanks to a new builder for the first three orders.
- Use this opportunity to do quotes, update files, gather materials for sales binders, etc.
- By staying in place for an extended period, you can set up appointments with those builders who have designated that means of contact rather than a cold call. Remember that current builders, customers, and prospective customers need to eat. Take advantage of the blocks of time in Figure 7.2 and buy them a meal. Breakfast allows for good conversation before the rush of the business day begins. If you choose to get together for lunch, try around 11:30 a.m. to avoid the rush.
- In the process of calling and setting up the week, you may come across a problem. Great! You are already in a situation-solving mode, and the builder will be impressed that you anticipated his or her need. You respond by saying, "Helen, I am sorry to hear that. What time could I stop by on Wednesday and look over what needs to be done? Do you want to meet at your office or at the jobsite?" You have established an immediate response to the need and have kept it in

FIGURE 7.2 Time Chart

WEEK

Time	Monday	Tuesday	Wednesday	Thursday	Friday
8:00					
10:00					
10:00					
12:00					
1:00					
3:00					
3:00					
5:00					
6:00					

your schedule. If Helen needs to see you before then, she'll let you know. Often the builder only wants your assurance that the situation is being addressed in a timely fashion.

■ As you plan your week, remind yourself that every stop needs a reason, not an excuse for gossip or chitchat. Have something of trade substance to say. You are taking the builder away from what he or she does for a living, so make it worth the time. Does the builder have a new need? Is evidence of an old problem returning? While you are on the site, take time to observe the house under construction. Do you have any ideas that might save the builder time? Have you read an article or observed a technique used elsewhere that this builder could use?

■ Record your progress toward meeting your goals.

■ Take advantage of before-business hours on Monday to fax, e-mail, write memos, and such before your telephone begins to ring. You will have the balance of your planning time to follow up on requests made during this time; in addition, your request will be ahead of those who wait until later in the day to call for help.

■ How long does it take you on average to go from stop to stop within one of the grids or zones in your territory? If it takes 25 minutes, for instance, then plan on that amount of time between stops and stay disciplined to the requirement. You will stay on schedule and avoid the extra pressure of being late.

As you allocate time, allow at least 15 to 30 minutes for each stop with a builder. Keep your calls to no more than 15 minutes; you can gather a great deal of information during that time. Figure 7.2 not only blocks the day into 2-hour grids, but allocates an hour around noon to be left open. Anticipate picking up lunch with a customer, prospect, or member of your network.

Try to avoid eating by yourself in your vehicle. That'll keep you from wearing your lunch in your lap or on your shirt or blouse, but you'll also digest your food better. If you've had a brutal morning, give yourself a break; 15 to 30 minutes spent on a meal should not slow you down. The break will do you good.

When blocking off time, recall any major issues you need to resolve for current builders that may require an hour or more. A scheduled visit with a major prospect should take nearly an hour. Do not overcommit.

If you volunteer to serve on a committee with your local home builders association, make sure the meeting will not last more than a hour. Save some energy for when you arrive back at home or the office. Take time to debrief yourself after the day and begin planning for the next one.

If you are also responsible for servicing the product, try to reserve a full day or two half days for completing the job. By controlling the time frame in which you perform these important tasks in a planned or prescribed manner, you create uninterrupted time to sell.

Territorial Management

With the judicious use of territory grids you can maintain regular contact with builders while having continued stops with prospects, all the time keeping your wits. There is one surefire time-consumer—builders that demand to see you now, regardless. You know who they are. You also know from experience that the problem does not necessarily require your immediate on-site attention. Often you can solve the crisis with a well-placed word to your company or to a source.

Use your best judgment when those calls come in. You could reply, "Thanks for bringing that to my attention, John. I will call my people or my contact immediately and get it resolved. If you need to know right away, then I will call you back as soon as I have an answer." or "What time tomorrow can I stop by and show or tell you what I have done?" That keeps you in your chosen activity for the rest of the day, avoids using up precious time running from one site to the other, and gives you nearly a day to come up with a solution.

For the sake of example, let's assume your sales or service territory can be broken down into at least four or five zones of approximately the same sales volume or number of active builders. A zone is no more than a compact area of your total territory, which allows you the versatility to react in a positive way with current as well as future builders in a specific geographic area. Try and work your sales/service territory without the use of zones, and you may find yourself tangled up with demands that require you to be in opposite parts of your territory at the same time. You should be able to work the zone on a regular basis in four and a half days a week (Figure 7.3).

You have set aside Monday morning for planning. Friday afternoon allows you to wrap-up, do last minute call backs, and finish other jobs needed by the builder before the weekend. Thursday could be reserved for touching base with builders in small-

FIGURE 7.3 Weekly Schedule

Monday	Tuesday	Wednesday	Thursday	Friday
a.m.—Planning p.m.—Zone 1	Zone 2	Zone 3	Zone 4 or 5	a.m.—Zone 1 p.m.—Zone 1 or loose ends

volume zones that do not require weekly contact. Or, you may want to consider using this day to develop a new zone.

By placing your sales in such zones, you are free to focus on that specific part of the territory. Your builders will tell you how often they need to see you; many will not need you on the jobsite each week

While in a particular zone, organize your schedule so you have time to see a sufficient number of prospects to meet your new account goal. A wise territorial manager will leave enough time for spontaneous contacts that occur when the manager is in a zone on a regular basis.

Put your daily time management scheme in a separate binder. That binder should contain a list of your current builders' key numbers and those of your vendors. Using current software, reduce most of this information to two sheets of paper or a screen in a handheld computer.

The first Monday in the month is an excellent day to update this information. Pass this update on to those people within your organization who are in touch with builders on a regular basis. Your daily log constitutes part of this simple but effective binder; keep the last 30 days for quick reference.

Figure 7.3 includes a copy of what you might use as part of this book; it can easily be adapted for your specific use. If you record events and contacts during the day, you can easily find the information when you need to recall numbers and details.

How do you keep track of what needs to happen in a day? You can find a large variety of proven time management systems on the market. Regardless of which one you use, consider augmenting it with a folder of the day. Use a different color for each day of the week.

The colored folders will make finding the right one easier when you go through your portable filing system. Each folder of the day will hold what you specifically need to do that day. As you pull together the week on Monday morning, place documents in the folders by the day they're needed. You may also want a separate file for expenses, so you can easily file your monthly report. Wise sales professionals keep handy quotes, contracts, credit applications, other assorted forms, and such in separate folders.

You can carry all this in a light, portable, 6-inch-deep by 9-inch-tall plastic box available at most office supply stores. Having all this information at your fingertips will make you more efficient in the field and will save time in the office, and it will expedite the sales cycle. A concise, compact system that is easy to use and maintain will add hours to your day.

If you are a trade contractor, the need to maximize the effectiveness of your planning is even more critical. If you work alongside your crews, your day begins quite early and often ends late. You may begin the day at the supply house picking up mate-

FIGURE 7.4 The Value of Your Time

To Earn Per Year	One Hour =	One Minute =	Wasted Time Cost 1 hr each day, yr
$35,000	$17.50	$.29	$4,375
$40,000	$20.00	$.33	$5,000
$45,000	$22.50	$.38	$5,625
$50,000	$25.00	$.42	$6,250
$60,000	$30.00	$.50	$7,500
$75,000	$37.50	$.63	$9,375
$85,000	$42.50	$.71	$10,625
$100,000	$50.00	$.83	$12,500
$125,000	$62.50	$1.04	$15,625
$150,000	$75.00	$1.25	$18,750
$175,000	$87.50	$1.46	$21,875
$200,000	$100.00	$1.67	$25,000

rial or by dispatching crews. These quiet hours before the bulk of the day allow you to provide positive input to your people. While headed to a job, make the cold call that is along your route. If you keep missing the prospective builder, rely on your network. Those people will be an excellent source of the best time or manner with which to contact the builder.

Figure 7.4 offers a few hints to help you in managing your time. One way you can use much of the material in carrying out effective territorial management can be found in the Chapter 8. Extend your efforts in selling to builders by creating and maintaining a strong network of trade contractors suppliers and builders. Good planning to you.

8

Build a Career-Friendly Network

The economy changes over time and so does the dynamics of the building industry. One of the forces that will effect this change will be trends that manifest themselves in other industries and then migrate to your back yard. To stay competitive in the marketplace your builders need to be prepared to meet the new demands brought on by trends.

As builders reshape their companies to respond to change, the size and type of builder businesses in your market will continually change. For example, let's say you're a market that has been made up of mostly small- to medium-volume builders. Within a short period of time, the more profitable medium-volume builders—and their land options—are purchased by out-of-state large-volume builders interested in establishing a base in your market.

Suddenly the dynamics of lots, lot prices, and product offerings have changed. So has the bidding process for trade contractors and suppliers. You can help guard against any adverse impacts from this change by establishing and growing a strong network. A network is a loosely formed group of people who share at least one common business interest. For businesses, networks create leads and a continuing source of information about the market. Everyone plays an equal part in the process.

You may not consider yourself part of a formal network, but you are if you hold membership in any local home builders association or other industry-related association. Many local home builders associations have an Associate Members Committee that represents the needs of associate members—those members who support builders with services and materials.

Some local associations have established formal leads groups as part of their Associate Members Committees. Check with your local home builders association staff for details. If your local association does not have a leads group, contact the staff of the Associate Members Committee of the National Association of Home Builders for a list of local associations that do. They should have details on how to begin to pull a leads group together.

Review several considerations when looking at leads. Initially you'll need to know where the lead originated. Some sources have higher credibility, hence their leads carry more weight when used. Next, consider how the lead was conveyed. Did the person who provided the lead convey a sense of urgency, or was it just a "fishing expedition" by a builder looking to keep his or her current supplier or trade contractor honest? You be the judge. Be the expediter who decides which lead needs immediate attention and which can wait for your weekly area rotation.

Keep the leads channel open and producing in five ways:

- Begin with the network itself; a solid and reliable network grows with time. It must be flexible enough to allow for others' career changes. Members have been known to change companies and even products while still maintaining their contacts in the building community. I have seen salespeople go from selling installed heating, ventilating and air conditioning air to insulation. Others have gone from selling appliances to selling windows and doors.

- Include like-minded people who share your goals and standards.

- Build the network around individuals whom you can trust. What they say and do and what you say and do must be 100 percent reliable. Your shared reputation in the building industry should be strong enough that when you invoke the reference's name in introducing yourself to a prospective builder, the reference's status will carry weight. The issue of reputation goes both ways. The reference implies that you are capable of performing at the level of the person who gave you the lead.

- Encourage diversity; a few members of your network will have regular contact with persons who participate in territories or areas that you currently do not serve. They may have contacts that would be useful to you. You in turn may be their prime informational contact in areas that they are not serving.

- Whenever you get a lead, follow up in a timely fashion. The manner in which you respond will encourage more leads in the future. Your attention to the lead will tell the person who gave you the contact that you value that person's confidence in you and that you have the skill and capacity to do a particular job for the builder.

- After completing a sales call, remember to thank the person in your network for the lead. Do something more if your networking friend helped you gain access to a number of builders or arranged an appointment with an important person inside a building company that you had pursued without success. A gift certificate to your networking friend's favorite restaurant would be appropriate. When adding people to your network, look for certain characteristics; you need to meet these same standards.

Characteristics of Reliable Network People

How can you tell if the people within your network are reliable? Look for these traits—

- They are willing to listen. Really listen. They take time to allow you to explain your business needs. They look for opportunities to share your name. You do likewise.
- They have the same business philosophy. Not everyone who sells to builders will do so with your same attitude. Beware of differences; make sure you feel comfortable with the manner in which these people conduct their businesses.
- You can trust them. If what they say is in fact not the truth, or their reputations are not up to your standards, the referral will be tainted in the builder's mind. The same needs to be said of you. What would builders you service think if they received a call from a prospective trade contractor or supplier who had been referred to them by you?
- They are held in high esteem in the building industry and/or community. In the building business, reputation lasts longer than image.

Regardless of whether the business atmosphere is strong or weak, your network can greatly assist you in finding and maintaining a strong presence in the building industry. Time spent developing the relationships that constitute your network will be time well invested in all of your futures. Leads are the lifeblood of a strong, consistently producing sales territory. They come in and allow you to meet the constant changes in the dynamic of your territory. Leads come from a diverse group of sources. How many are you using?

A Resource Schedule For Leads

- Builders who hold what you do in high esteem can provide powerful leads. In the recent survey conducted in conjunction with the writing of this book, builders said the second most important source for a new supplier or trade contractor was a referral from a respected colleague.

Your network within and beyond the local home builders association offers a prime source for knowing who is doing what and where. Next to information from a builder, a network provides your most powerful leads. Those leads will come from someone who knows you, your company, and your ability to perform. If the building community respects this person, the name will carry great weight. Use it.

"Mr. Builder, I was speaking with Joe the plumber last night at the meeting of the local home builders association, and he mentioned that you are looking for a good framing crew. We have worked on a variety of homes over the last two years. Joe knows our work well because we share several builders in common. He asked me to mention his name when I called."

- If you work with a national manufacturer that uses magazine ads and direct mail to market to consumers interested in building or remodeling their homes, the manufacturer may supply occasional leads. Your regional representative serves as the normal conduit. If you represent a nationally known brand name, the manufacturer should pass leads on through regional managers. Trade publications are filled with national ads that offer 800 numbers, e-mail addresses, and reply cards for builders to use. Your regional representative normally will pass the lead along.

- If your company produces local marketing campaigns directed at builders or consumers, provide swift follow-up for the leads.

- Some trade shows limit attendance to builders, industry professionals, and others who work to reach and educate homeowners. Look for leads that can be used to pull or push business through to the builder.

- McGraw-Hill Publishing produces the Dodge Report series, which lists current starts for a variety of building activities in markets ranging from single-family to heavy commercial. If your firm subscribes, you will receive notice of coming projects and have access to the plan room that contain specifications and plans. This service is available across the country. Check your local telephone directory.

- Many locales have their own version of housing starts information. Some regional services exist as well. Check with your local home builders association, Chamber of Commerce, and Better Business Bureau for such local sources.

- The telephone directory gives only a general sense of who is building in the area. Most builders do not advertise in the back section of the telephone book

- Your local home builders association's membership list presents an excellent source for leads. Ask the association staff for insight into sales volumes and possible important contacts within the organization. It will give you a great beginning to a mailing list. The home builders association will update the list on a regular basis.

- Canvassing your territory can reveal more names. Jot down information from signs in the front yards and from building permit boxes that populate most jobsites.

- Former customers are a good source of leads; approach them correctly and you may regain their business. You may now offer more products or services that they could use.

- Let the world know what you do for a living; you'd be surprised at the number of people you know who may need their homes remodeled or want to have a house built. This information provides a valuable introduction to a builder. You are bringing him or her a lead.

- During your career you will also meet people who will become part of your circle of friends who know builders. My experience says they will have contact with builders who you may not have successfully reached. They can provide an introduction over breakfast or lunch.

- The reference desks at many local libraries contain lists of businesses by type. Compiled on a statewide basis, these lists are often a year old but can still provide names for you to contact.

- Any retail business (grocery, hardware store, and the like) that has a bulletin board will usually have at least one builder on the board. Your local lumberyard or home center should have lots of names.

- You will have at least one builder-savvy real estate agent in your market who knows who is building where. Get to know this person. What can you do to help the agent get more listings?
- Check with your local home builders association or library for a listing of licensed builders in your state. This list may be a year old. If you are interested in selling to small-volume builders, the list is an excellent source for finding those who stay busy in out-of-the-way markets. If you wish to purchase the list, contact your state licensing board.
- What kind of relationship do you have with developers in your territory? They are pulling together the land for tomorrow's houses. You may want to assist them in finding builders as they promote your business.
- Newspaper ads. Every week one issue of your local paper will feature builders and remodelers; be sure to read that feature. Keep track of who appears in the paper and what services each choose to feature as their best work.
- Follow a competitor's delivery trucks.
- When driving through developments, look for the builder's sign. If you don't see any (and many do not put signs in the yard), check the building permit box.
- As mentioned earlier, trade contractors working on the job can be a great source of information. The longer the trade contractor has worked for the builder, the more credible the information.
- Blind calls or drop-bys at your office. These builders or associates are curious about what you do. Show them.
- Local promotional events such as open houses and local home shows provide excellent avenues for building your network and collecting leads. If you host one of these events, invite current and prospective members to your place of business or to the show site.
- If you have a respectful relationship with your competitor, at some point this person may realize that he or she cannot serve the particular need of a specific builder. If you have a solid reputation in the industry and offer that product, your competitor may come to you with that lead and a wealth of information on how to meet the builder's needs. Builders can even become customers from such circumstances.
- Tabletop nights at the home builders association provide a relaxed atmosphere to show what you do, often in close proximity to your competitor. Builders can easily compare and see how good you are. Why not send your current builders a personal invitation to come see your company's new offerings. Suggest they bring a friend.
- Strategic alliances. Simply put, these groups are gatherings of companies or trade contractors that are losing selling opportunities to much larger companies. Strategic alliances allow each company to do what it does best, in concert with one another.
- Eat where the builders eat. Most areas have a restaurant or two where builders and trade contractors gather to eat breakfast and lunch. Know them, frequent them. Use the restaurant as part of a promotional strategy; you buy breakfast or lunch there every so often to gather leads.

- Consult your telephone directory for the names of companies that specialize in direct mail. Often they can create and fulfill mailings to builders of whom you may not be aware.
- Consider purchasing specialized mailing list software. Many choices are available from your local computer outlet.

A builder who likes what you sell but cannot make use of it at that time may be a great source for leads. Ask for the names of builders who might be interested in your products or services. "Thank you, Mr. Builder for telling me that you cannot use my product right now. Your enthusiasm seems to be real. Do you know another builder in this area who could use my service or product?" They do and often will give you some leads. Be sure and ask if you may use the builder's name in your introduction.

- Several builder-associate related groups have formed as part of local home builders associations. These networking opportunities are built around breakfasts or bag lunches. After a brief word of welcome, the facilitator allows associates a 30-second explanation of who they are, what they do, and what classification of business they are seeking. Some have gone so far as to ask for contacts with a specific builder. A featured builder often speaks at these type of meetings. The builders give a brief history of who they are and how they got into the business.

Often they will tell attendees what they are looking for in trade or suppliers. Some of these networking groups allow members to give 5-minute talks about what they do, supply, apply, and install. The leads are often tracked using a two-part carbonless form (Figure 8.1). The Greater Greensboro (North Carolina) Builders Association, classi-

FIGURE 8.1 Leads Notice

Date: _____

Lead to: _____

Lead from: _____ Title: _____

Contact: _____

Company: _____

Address: _____

City: _____

Telephone: _____

Note: _____

_____

fied as a medium-size home builders association, facilitates over a thousand leads a year in such a format.

All this takes time. When I moved to my present location I arrived without knowing anyone except my employer. Over the past seven years I have developed a network that has seen people come and go. Some have become friends and my partners in profit. I count among the group two Realtors®, several builders or remodelers, a siding applicator, a trim supplier, a painting contractor, an owner of a medium-sized lumberyard, two investment bankers, one retail banker, several home builders association staff members, a house designer, an appliance salesperson, an insurance broker, and a caterer. It was not built overnight; few things that are worthwhile are. These relationships take time to build and maintain. They are the keys to your future.

9

Working with Large-Volume Builders

In Chapter 6 you learned strategies for contacting and submitting proposals to large-volume builders. This chapter will show you the most effective way to work with these builders.

As you approach these potentially valuable accounts, remember to follow some basic guidelines: Do you really want the business? Obtaining business at this volume involves hidden costs. How hungry for the business are you, and are you prepared to do what is necessary as a trade contractor or supplier to close the transaction? Other questions you need to answer are—

How important would this potential business be to yours? Is this potential account a matter of volume of dollars or prestige? Would it be a strong addition to your profit or just more market share? The paragraphs that follow discuss some of the hidden costs of doing business with large-volume builders.

Consider:

Communication. Depending on whether you deliver a product or a service, are all parts of your company properly connected? In some cases you'll need an inside or perhaps outside sales coordinator to serve as a clearing center for all activity on the account. You may fill the same capacity as well. The key is making sure all parts of your organization talk often to each other about the builder's daily concerns. Daily contact will greatly aid in eliminating duplication of calls, deliveries, installation crews, and such.

Infrastructure. You will need a sufficiently strong infrastructure in place to handle the added demands—and the problems that can arise. Do you have the necessary people, building, and vehicles available to meet the demands before you secure the account? Consider establishing a separate work team to handle these builders' unique demands. This team would function as part of your entire company but would be dedicated to meeting the needs of this specific account. As part of this team you may want to consider setting up a separate accounting scheme as well. Larger builders normally buy products and services at rates substantially lower than their smaller counterparts.

Capital. Do you have sufficient resources available to support the necessary increases in labor or inventory? Builders at this volume will often pay on a weekly basis for labor-intensive jobs, but will expect discounts in return. The most accurate accounting of your true costs can come only by breaking out the fixed and variable cost of doing business at this level. Doing business just for the sake of doing business makes no sense. Do you have the necessary capital available to sustain the level of service you'll need to meet this size builder's demanding schedule? Builders at this level are concerned about the strength of those they deal with; assure them you can handle their business now and will be strong enough to service them in the future.

Contact. Be careful not to leave your smaller builders behind in the dust you created as you scrambled to meet the larger builders' growing demands. With a strong plan (such as the one suggested in Chapter 7), you can maintain proper, consistent contact with all your builders. If this becomes a problem, you may need to add sales or service people to maintain an acceptable level of service to all builders.

Not all companies have the discipline or resources necessary to meet the unique demands of selling to large-volume builders. What looks good on paper becomes a very real trap if you cannot meet demands. Having trade contractors and suppliers coming and going is not in the best interests of a large-volume builder. The sheer number of houses constructed demands uniformity in materials and workmanship.

Expect builders at this level to ask for you to lock in your price. This expectation may be centered on a time period (such as one year from the agreement) or will be specific to a project. They will carefully monitor what you charge. There is no room for invoice creep. The bidding process is time consuming for you and the builder. Level pricing for goods and services saves time as well as money.

In spite of the number of houses being constructed, builders at this volume still care about quality. You will work hard to get their business. Work as hard taking care of the small issues that arise that keep your quality of goods and services at the top.

Usually large-volume builders are organizationally conscious. They tend to have an established hierarchy both in the office and in the field. Find out how decisions are made and by whom. Builders of this sales volume size keep a published list of telephone and cell phone numbers for internal use.

This usually confidential list would be most helpful. The gatekeeper can be of great assistance in making sure the information you seek or need to have distributed gets to the proper person in a timely manner. Be prepared to conduct business the way their system needs to. Adapt to their procedures/policies. This is critical to the amount of paper usually generated by such an account.

Builders at this volume often have several key people that you will need to be in contact with regularly. Assume that the Purchasing Manager will be your regular line of communication; this person usually follows the trail of the sale from installation to invoice and then payment. All procedural changes on your part normally should start with this person. An increasing number of large-volume builders use Project Managers, who are responsible for tracking everything involved with a particular project. Builders who are constructing attached single-family buildings often employ project managers. Issues with pricing, availability of product and installation, specifications, and such need to be channeled through this person.

Large-volume builders will also use some type of estimator. This person coordinates the introduction of new products and services to the line of homes offered. Often they are computer-savvy with strong experience in actual home construction. Be sure to contact this key person with any changes in what you have available.

Because of long-term commitments to the community, large-volume builders maintain a warranty department. The size of the staff will vary, but depend on this department to look after your product or service after the contract with the new homeowner closes. You may be called upon to repair whatever you have supplied or installed; be cognizant of the mandated response time this department has promised to homeowners. Chapter 10 contains suggestions for responding to homeowners' needs.

Be prepared to attend lots of meetings. Builders at this volume often hold weekly production meetings with key personnel and may require that you attend. If so, do you have the time? If not, can someone in your organization represent you and answer the tough questions that often come up in a high production-based building environment? Depending on the organization's make-up, you may need to also stay in touch on a regular basis with its estimating, purchasing, accounting, customer service, and other departments.

Large-volume builders practice a disciplined approach to the purchase of goods and services. Chapter 6 describes how to approach the professional purchasing manager. Once you have the account, you must adapt your system to how the builders run theirs. They will have some form of purchase order or start release form that gives you permission to do what you do. You will need to adhere to their billing requirements. Part of their requirements will be to reference the job by name and address. They may require that you sign on one of their forms as part of their billing procedure. The larger the firm, the more rigid the requirements if you want to be paid in a timely fashion. Stray from the builder's preset guidelines and expect delays in being paid. All the hoops that trade contractors and suppliers have to jump through are needed as safeguards for the builder.

Large-volume builders operate many developments. Often they keep these multiple sites going in a scattered pattern based on market trends, availability of lots, sewer and water lines, and such. Take time to see where they are currently building, then ask about their future plans. Once you have this information, you'll need to answer these questions:

- Are you prepared or able to service their needs at the same level as your current builder base?
- Are you prepared to add staff or inventory to meet those needs?
- Have you taken these and other related measures into account in your cost?

Builders of this size need lots of TLC—be prepared to administer it. You have little room for error. Large-volume builders often use plans that are well established regarding what products and services they require and when they need them. They have a set schedule, and your jobsite contact is under pressure from day one to meet an already established closing date. A 2,000-square-foot home can easily be up and occupied in less than 90 days; at this speed there's no margin for error.

Do not be surprised to share a portion of what you install/apply or supply with one of your competitors. Large-volume builders are less likely than their smaller cousins to put all their eggs in one basket. You may be assigned to a style of housing (as in townhouses only or cluster homes) or a geographical section of the market.

They also have no tolerance for excuses as to why a product was not delivered or a service not performed. All stages build on one another. The timelines are so tight and margins so thin that everybody must hit their mark or the whole process slows. The product or service you bring to the builder doesn't matter. You have to maintain the established schedule or lose the business. Be creative as you work around the schedules of others who are not sensitive to builders' time demands and, of course, the weather.

You and your employees will need to be up to speed on the technical aspects of what you install/apply or supply. At the volume these companies build, there is little room for lapses in technique or training. If a part is left off or is not installed properly, then it could in fact impact hundreds of houses in short order. To meet the demands of a massive recall of a defective part of the house could be devastating to the reputation and viability of the trade contractor or supplier and tarnish the name of the builder. Be wise. Know your product well.

Builders at this volume expect you to treat them as if they were your only customer. They want it now—not tomorrow. Know the expectations going in. Ask trade contractors and suppliers who are currently doing business or key contacts you trust within the organization.

You know doubt smile when you look at the number of houses that a builder at this level constructs in a year. Unless you are currently doing business with them, you need to realize that the volume often comes in spurts. Housing starts may revolve around seasonal promotions, local home builders association's Parade of Homes, and such. The starts do not normally come in neat tidy amounts. Often it is feast or famine. You will need to make sure your business stays busy and profitable when the large-volume builder is between spurts. Develop a good relationship with the sales staff to keep yourself abreast of future demand.

The sheer size of the account should not bother you if you have the necessary infrastructure in place. Simply consider the number of developments that will be added to your territory as individual new builder accounts and call on them accordingly.

The larger the company, the more critical your role with your own company. If you are part of a large company as well, your services will often be required as an ombudsman between the two parties. The stronger the paper flow, the larger the number of opportunities for something to be entered or noted incorrectly. Sometimes you will be called upon to link interested parties together.

One large-volume builder reminded me that his company along with the trade contractor and supplier has one aim in mind: produce a quality product that will please the homeowner. The bottom line is that everyone works for the home buyer.

Because of the intense pressure that can come from multiple houses built in a single development by a one builder, be prepared to react with a sense of urgency when problems arise. Depending on what you supply or install, you may need to have a 24/7 number and trained staff. There are systems that are sensitive to time and temperature. Electrical, HVAC, roofing, and plumbing are among the most critical. If you fall within these areas, be prepared. If the purchasing manager does not ask during your presentation whether you have the capability for immediate service, bring it up.

Experience has taught me that the industry has three basic types of large-volume builders.

Family-Style Builders. Large-volume family-run building businesses usually have been around for more than one generation. This type of builder maintains a great deal of loyalty to trade contractors, suppliers, and his or her staff. This builder experiences little turnover in any of these groups because they are loyal in return. This loyalty means that you will have a tough time getting any of their business and connections may be crucial. Once in, as long as you continue to meet their standards, you'll be the often promoting from within. The punch-out person 20 years ago may be the purchasing manager or the production manager today. You and your staff may be invited to attend family-style events that could include picnics, trips to see sporting events, golf, or fishing outings.

Family-Style But No Longer Family-Owned Builders. The second style of larger-volume builder was a family business similar to the first one but one that has been bought by an aggressive national or dominant regional firm. Companies that purchase family building businesses on a local basis wisely recognize the asset they have purchased and leave them alone. Expect few changes. When those changes do come they'll be broad, as in the need to cut costs in a certain area department or building phase or to be more uniform in another to meet a standard dictated by the corporate office. The change in ownership presents strong possibilities to do more business. If you have been excluded because of product lines that you carry and you find the new owner uses them in other locations, suggest that these products are available to the local operation through you.

Pace-Driven Builders. The last large-volume builder always seems to be in turmoil. You will see changes in staff all along the organization. Builders and sales staff often last just over a year and are burned out by the pace. Those employees who can adapt will thrive; you'll see them rise rapidly in the organization. There's little room for sentiment here. Price and service come first in these firms.

There's little room for loyalty, either and because the pace of production is so fierce, those who make purchasing decisions often rotate as well. Be certain that they replace products or services with like products and services. Stay in touch with those making the buying decisions and stay abreast of trends in products and services in your area of expertise. The positive people contacts you make and maintain will serve you well in the future. As the turnover comes, you'll find friends going to other companies that perhaps you have been unable to do business with in the past. If so, you will have someone inside the organization who knows you can do the job.

Basically, the three types of large-volume builders all are focused on one thing: turning out a large number of high quality homes at a rapid pace. Large-volume builders require a lot of work on your part, but they can be profitable long-term customers. See if supplying this market would prove profitable for you.

10

Some Last Thoughts

This chapter is devoted to bits and pieces of wisdom that offer a substantial pay-off in selling to builders. No one subject justifies a chapter by itself but each has sufficient importance that it merits your attention.

When the Wheels Fall Off

If you recall, the early portion of Chapter 2 guides you as you establish your purpose and goals and then bring them to life. Setting goals helps keep you focused on what's important and gives you a reference point for the remainder of the year. This information was designed to give you direction and a gentle push into taking advantage of all that positive energy that flows during the beginning of a year, either calendar or fiscal.

What happens when you arrive at the beginning of the second quarter not even close to being on track with your goals? "Steve," you say, "I have had so many distractions, the weather has been horrible, and for several days I needed to devote my time to family matters. Where has the year gone?"

How is your year going? As you measure your progress toward those noble and enabling goals, are you on track? Are the goals still reasonable? Is the fact that they are specific keeping you on task? If you answer yes to all four questions and yet are considerably behind in the game, somewhere along the way the wheels have fallen off your little red wagon. What do you do? Start by congratulating yourself; you have taken the first step toward getting back on course with this acknowledgment.

You have a problem, but you do have time to recover. By reviewing the three steps in formulating goals (measurable, reasonable, specific) you have determined that they are not the problem. What is? An improper sense of urgency could be the culprit; it arrives in the slyest of ways through the innocent request of bosses, friends, builders, even family. Just when you are organized and on the move people call or show up, and you are off chasing "rabbits" for them. You don't need to become rude and run off kin and clients, but in a diplomatic manner let them know you are in the middle of a project or assignment and would love to help but cannot until you finish the work at hand. You may want to designate a time or place to be left alone to carry out your daily requirements in fulfilling your goals.

Sensing my need for privacy in the midst of telephone calls and hot-and-cold running teenagers, my wife created an "occupied" hat band. This simple ring fits over a variety of hats and boldly proclaims, "OCCUPIED." It tells all that come close that I am on task. If I am alone, I let the telephone ring and let the machine pick up the call. I get that goal-centered chore done, return the phone call, and then I go on about the day.

Review your goals daily. Post them in a prominent place. Create charts to record progress (as in sales history, actual versus projected). You need to know where you are right now and where you need to be. Regular review keeps goals in focus and in mind.

I am often asked by others who observe my schedule, "How do you get it all done?" Simple. I don't always accomplish everything I plan, but I finish things that are most critical in pursuing my goals.

You and I are sometimes required to be at several locations at or near the same time. Laws of physics tell us that we cannot, even with cell phones and e-mail. However, these and other electronic devices can allow us to communicate en route and reschedule. Your relentless pursuit of your goals will determine where you need to be most.

Keep your anxiety down when fighting feelings of urgency, and stay on task to continue steady progress toward your goals. If they are worthy of your energy and talent, they deserve your best effort.

Builders or associates who interrupt the process through their own lack of planning or lack of goals can learn from your example. Stay focused and follow through. Watch how making steady progress toward completing your goals makes them come to life. Figure 2.6 shows a form that has been used successfully by others. The form allows you to record daily progress on 1-, 3-, and 5-year goals. Use this form in good wealth and health, and put the wheels back on your little red wagon.

"Wow, We Do Have a Problem"

Problems that develop in your business will not be as dramatic as a NASA spacecraft crisis or emergency brain surgery, but when you're in the middle of a swamp surrounded by alligators, no one cares who forgot to drain the swamp. You have a problem. What do you do? How you react to problems that come up says much to your customers about your problem-solving skills as well your company's commitment to making life easier for them.

This section examines the issue of problem solving and presents traditional and nontraditional means of responding to problems. First off, realize that no matter how hard you and a builder may try in constructing a house, problems can occur. If things are quiet at the office, and your customer service people are taking two-hour lunches, watching soap operas before and after lunch, and reading long, boring novels during the day, you know business with builders is slow.

Challenges that arise during the construction process often result from a builder having difficulty outside the job, his or her customer becoming too involved in the building process, or a customer service issue creating a worse problem. The more expensive a building project becomes, the more personal the level of involvement you can expect from the homeowner.

Problems result when a breakdown occurs in communication between the builder and the homeowner. When both parties don't get together to discuss what is happening at the job, look out. The frustration of a customer trying to contact the builder may be carried to the jobsite, and it can fall into your lap as trade contractor or salesperson. The problem may be one of interpretation: "The builder said that you wanted the windows to be here, while the original plans indicate them here."

Other questions that arise regarding the building of the house include the colors of walls, exterior surfaces, floor coverings, styles of cabinets, landscaping, layouts of rooms, and the like. The problem may be just a simple lack of communication, but the supplier and trade contractor end up in the middle. Companies that provide good customer service and that listen and react in a positive manner become the focal point for the homeowner.

Problems with the house may well disguise something that occurs at a much deeper level. Some few years ago our company was faced with a particular customer service problem that seemed only to get worse with time. Every time my company sent its service people and performed a repair to everyone's satisfaction, the homeowner would call to have us return. After this happened on several occasions, the complaint was referred to me.

I called the service people who had made the in-home visits and then the homeowner. The problem was not with the product but with the situation. Our customer's husband was suffering from a terminal illness, and her frustration over her inability to do anything about the illness was at the center of her anger.

My company became the focal point for that anger. Each time we responded to her calls with a new product. For those few minutes when she was talking with a customer service person or a technician, she was able to avoid what was occurring in the next room.

The problem is not always the problem. If you have done all that you can do to resolve the issue, think beyond the obvious and consider that it may not be you or your product at all.

It's vital that you maintain clear lines of communication with the builder. Experience has shown that builders can handle the truth but don't do too well with surprises or information vacuums. If a situation that you or the builder did not anticipate arises, get the word to the builder immediately. Keep accurate notes of what you see or do.

The use of faxes or e-mail enhances your ability to get time-sensitive information to the builder and provides a record of your actions simultaneously. If the homeowner is involved in decisions and the builder is not, pass the results as quickly as possible to the builder. The more that you have in writing, such as change orders or special requests from the homeowner, the easier resolution will be. Problems rarely solve themselves or go away quietly.

Anticipate possible problems or bottlenecks. The building process moves quickly and involves many people in just the construction phase. If you can imagine that something may go wrong or you have seen it happen in the past, plan for it. Have back-up stock, crews to work extra hours, exotic parts within short distances.

Often the small parts and pieces drive the builder's frustration level. The extra crown mold piece in the corner of the dining room, the missing light fixture in the master bath, the bracket that holds the filter on the range hood, a bad balance in a window, a cupped deck board. Anticipate these incidents and respond to them during your regular visits to the job. Make the problem disappear before it becomes an issue.

Simple Steps to Solving Problems

You will find listed below some easy steps to take in solving problems:

- Gather all the information you can find. The more information, the better the base for finding a solution.
- Devote your time and energy to finding a solution rather than looking for someone or some circumstance to blame. Builders are interested in performance, not excuses.
- Brainstorm with all parties who have an interest in making the situation disappear. If all the affected parties are together, no one has anyone to blame.
- Move with a sense of urgency, based on the words of the builder. Does it have to be solved today, really today, or do you have two days to make it happen? The resources that are available to you will affect that decision.
- Be truthful, consistent, and keep all involved parties informed. People affected by the problems are more often interested in the "dos" of the situation than they are the "whys." So do.
- Feel free to consult with other trade contractors or suppliers about the situation. The solution may rest in someone else's experience in a nonrelated field. When you find a solution, make the necessary changes in procedure or products to keep it from occurring again.
- If this problem is industry-wide, ask what others are doing to resolve the issue. What can you learn from them? What can they learn from you?
- If the situation impacts other trade contractors or suppliers, make sure they are in the information loop.
- Be creative. If prior attempts to solve the problem have failed, then do something different. View a problem as an opportunity to show how good you and your people are.

You can be most creative when you leave old solutions behind and press forward. If several people are involved in solving the issue, get together and look at possibilities beyond what has been tried in the past.

Do that by beginning to think in extremes. For instance, you may have difficulty meeting early morning delivery schedules for several builders. All the builders want their product on the job first, but your company has only one truck and the truck and driver can only be at one site at a time.

Begin the problem-solving exercise by thinking in the extreme. Have you thought of using blimps or helicopters? How about having the material beamed aboard a spaceship and then sent to the jobsite in a near-instant? Extreme? All three solutions are fantasies, but they may suggest a germ of possibility using conventional means such as delivering the evening before. Be creative.

- Solving an issue in a positive way will create great good will with the builder and, if a homeowner is involved, that person as well. Both can become strong referral sources.
- Try and create solutions that benefit both parties.
- If extra costs are involved, do not hesitate to share them with the people affected by the problem and the solution.

You have gathered all the information you can gather. You have done everything that you or your company can do to address the situation. You have kept everyone informed along the way. Make a decision and execute the process; don't look back. Once you reach a resolution, make sure all parties are aware of what was done and when. Be sure and cover any long-term effects with the affected parties. Communication rules.

Time Is Everything

The need for you to be sensitive to time and its impact on builders was first mentioned in Chapter 1. During at least two other periods in the building of a house a builder becomes even more sensitive to the ticks on the clock.

The most vulnerable times in the building process seem to be during the framing stage and 72 hours before closing. During the framing stage many elements, trade contractors, and suppliers must come together to get the house dried in. In many parts of the country the house in this stage of construction has to have a variety of materials and products installed for the building inspector to allow the process to continue. If the house does not pass inspection, time becomes an even more relentless enemy. During some parts of the year the house remains open to the caprices of weather, playing havoc on budgets and time lines to closing.

The second most vulnerable time comes during those last frantic days before the sale of the house is closed. Experience has taught me that the last 72 hours are critical. These last three days are when finishing touches, long-delayed repairs, and last-minute changes from the builder come into play. Be prepared to react in a positive and timely manner to any needs regarding your product. Keep items that seem to get misplaced, broken, bent, or scratched in stock and ready for immediate shipment or installation. It's your chance to shine and be a real hero in the eyes of the builder.

Set Limits: When Enough Is Enough

Chapter 2 explains the need to be persistent in pursuit of the sale. When you consider how best to manage your territory, another element comes into play: the customer who can never be satisfied. You have probably called on this type of builder; some of us sell to this type on a regular basis. The relationship began with great expectations on your part; it looked like the beginning of a great partnership. Your goods, services, and price allowed your expectations to be compatible with those of the builder. A high comes with a new account.

Those first sales look good on the sales report, more service stops to record for your monthly activity report or for a trade contractor, a picture of the completed job makes your presentation folder fatter. Then things begin to change.

You begin to realize that this isn't really a partnership at all. It lacks the mutual respect or commitment needed for both parties to prosper; this customer consistently demands more and more of you. Being a conscientious salesperson or trade contractor, you try to meet the builder's growing expectations. If he or she wants you to be at the office every Tuesday at 6:34 a.m., you are there on time. You may go the extra mile and show up with a smile and a box of doughnuts. Then you're asked to be there two days a week and bring coffee. Demands on the jobsite are the same. Your trade may have to cover the slack effort of another trade without being paid for your time and effort. When you approach the builder, he or she informs you that that is just part of your job.

If the volume of the business and the income become great enough to warrant such treatment, then bake the doughnuts at home or volunteer to cover the tracks of more trades. But if the demands are more and more and the results are less and less, take a reality break and ask yourself: "Is this expenditure of energy and time worth the pay back? Is it the best and most profitable use of my time?"

If you are not the sole owner of your business, this situation might provide an opportunity to bring the next level of management into the picture to look for a solution to this dilemma. A few builders will find good reliable people like you and ride you for as long as you can go, and when you stop to catch your breath, replace you. A few builders may harbor the feeling that your price runs too high and your service is not good enough. Neither was that of the trade contractor or supplier you replaced. This builder may be the one you took from your competitor with great pricing or promises of super service. When price becomes the sole motivating factor, selling is over. How low do you want to go? The customer may see no bottom.

Veteran salespersons or tradespeople have learned over the years that even if given the product or service, some customers would still consider the price too high. If that becomes the case, make a wise business decision and discontinue the relationship. That type of customer has no interest in long-term relationships or the strengths they bring to his or her business. Be gentle when you leave, for two reasons. One, he or she still could be an outlet for surplus material that you need to clear from inventory. Two, keep the window open; the builder may see the light and change.

Making the Most of Your Local Home Builders Association Membership

Builder sales contacts are not necessarily confined to their offices or jobsites. Networking opportunities with builders exist through your local professional builders